1987

SEX, POLITICS, AND SCIENCE
IN THE NINETEENTH-CENTURY NOVEL

Selected Papers from the English Institute
New Series

Sex, Politics, and Science
in the Nineteenth-Century Novel

 Selected Papers from the English Institute, 1983–84

New Series, no. 10

Edited by Ruth Bernard Yeazell

THE JOHNS HOPKINS UNIVERSITY PRESS
BALTIMORE AND LONDON

The Johns Hopkins University Press,
701 West 40th Street, Baltimore, Maryland 21211
The Johns Hopkins Press, Ltd, London

The paper in this book is acid-free and meets the guidelines for permanence
and durability of the Committee on Production Guidelines for Book Lon-
gevity of the Council on Library Resources.

Library of Congress Cataloging-in-Publication Data
Main entry under title:

Sex, politics, and science in the nineteenth-century
    novel.

    (Selected papers from the English Institute;
1983-84, new ser., no. 10)
    1. English fiction—19th century—History and
criticism—Addresses, essays, lectures.   2. American
fiction—19th century—History and criticism—Addresses,
essays, lectures.   3. Sex in literature—Addresses,
essays, lectures.   4. Literature and society—
Addresses, essays, lectures.   I. Yeazell, Ruth Bernard.
II. Series: Selected papers from the English Institute;
new ser., no. 10.
PR871.S49   1985   823'.8'09   85-45043
ISBN 0-8018-3059-1 (alk. paper)

Contents

Introduction

These essays take the nineteenth-century novel seriously by not treating it as privileged—by directing attention, in other words, to the language and systems of representation that it shared with the wider culture, and to the more or less open ways in which it participated in that culture. If the authors are not as obviously engaged with the poetics of fiction as they might have been a decade ago, they are perhaps more alert to the fictiveness of discourse generally, and to the anxieties that any fiction may manipulate and conceal. The volume opens with a detailed study of *Barchester Towers* and closes with a reading of "The Beast in the Jungle," but D. A. Miller and Eve Kosofsky Sedgwick approach these familiar works with a certain healthy suspicion: by looking for the police in Trollope or the homoeroticism in James, they compel the reader to see what is significantly not-present— or at least remains well hidden—in the text. And it is a sign of the collective project represented here that Trollope and James share these pages not only with George Eliot and Hardy, or with Bram Stoker and James M. Barrie, but with nineteenth-century economists and evolutionary biologists, with psychiatrists, sociologists, and even obstetricians.

This volume had its origins in a session on feminist biography at the 1983 meeting of the English Institute and a session devoted to new perspectives on the nineteenth-century novel the following year. At the former, Catherine Gallagher spoke on the metaphor of writing as prostitution in *Daniel Deronda*, while Eve Kosofsky Sedgwick contributed a paper that has since been published elsewhere and is replaced here by the new piece on James and homosexual panic. D. A. Miller's and Gillian Beer's papers were first delivered at the 1984 session, while Elaine

Showalter's and Mark Seltzer's papers were specially commissioned for this volume. This sequence of events is not as arbitrary as it might seem, for feminist critics were among the first to urge both a return to history and a skeptical questioning of canonical texts, as well as to pursue the implications of literary silence and oblivion. The influence of Michel Foucault's suspicious account of the history of power, of science, and of sexuality can also be noted behind a number of the essays—though as he himself might well have argued, it is impossible to sort out such individual "influence" from those more widely diffused shifts of attention that mysteriously manifest themselves at a particular historical moment.

D. A. Miller's essay on *Barchester Towers* offers the most extensive reading of a single novel in the collection, but as his finely ironic title suggests, he takes Trollope's famous work as a representative case: in the very "normality" of its imagined world and of its fictional procedures (what James called Trollope's "complete appreciation of the usual"), Miller detects the thoroughness with which conflict is managed and defused, the almost terrifying effectiveness of a system that has rendered overt police power unnecessary. In Miller's subtle interpretation, "moderate schism" characterizes not only Barchester's religious struggles but its sexual politics, and extends as well to the very structure of the Trollopean personality and the typically defusing operations of the Trollopean plot. Miller's argument reaches beyond Barchester and even "the Novel as Usual" to "the bourgeois liberal tradition of thought" with which the novel was so closely allied.

Catherine Gallagher also uses a single novel to illuminate a much larger problem—the anxieties of female authorship in the nineteenth century. The metaphor of the writer as prostitute, she argues, is at least as venerable as that of the writer as father—though no less threatening, obviously, to women seeking to enter the literary marketplace. Analyzing the association between the idea of prostitution and that of usury, and tracing the curious interrelations and exchanges among the figures of the prostitute, the usurer, and the artist in *Daniel Deronda,* Gallagher describes George Eliot's struggle to counter the perceived danger, her ambivalent effort to replace an unproductive system of exchange with a "moral economy." Though George Eliot's unsanctioned relation with George Henry Lewes rendered her particularly vulnerable to such anxieties, the fear of prostituting oneself through publication is clearly not limited to unmarried women; in conjunction with the nineteenth-century homosexual panic that Sedgwick later analyzes, Gallagher's suggestive essay does much to explain the anxieties of men like Hawthorne or James, who also suffered ambivalence about entering the "degradingly female" territory of the nineteenth-century novel.

In "Origins and Oblivion in Victorian Narrative," Gillian Beer addresses a form of anxiety at once universally human and historically particular to the nineteenth century, whose collective consciousness was newly awakened to the terrifying vastness of earth's unrecorded time. Explicitly refusing to treat literature as foreground and all other writing as mere "background," Beer instead calls attention to the exchanges of metaphor and idea between them: her essay deliberately juxtaposes texts from Sir Charles Lyell, Darwin, and Hardy, or from Dickens, Max Müller, and Freud. Both in scientific narratives and in avowedly fictive ones, Beer finds evidence of the Victorians' intensified sense of evanescence—and of their efforts to counter oblivion by insisting on the recovery of signs and traces. While the geologists searched for the intermittent "writing" on the rocks, the novelists repeatedly represented the quest for lost origins; and at the close of the century, the psychoanalysts took as their premise the unconscious storing of memory. At once so long and complex as inevitably to induce forgetting and sternly insistent that the reader keep track of moral and causal connection, the Victorian multiplot novel serves Beer as but one model for the divided impulses of the age.

Elaine Showalter, in "Syphilis, Sexuality, and the Fiction of the Fin de Siècle," also focuses on the Victorian obsession with signs left by the past, but the hysteria of which she writes concentrated on the threat of devolution rather than evolution, and the signs that were to be deciphered lay not in the fossil record but in the visible ravages of human flesh. Arguing that syphilis was *the* symbolic disease of the fin de siècle, the metaphoric focus of the decade's virulent anxieties about sexuality, heredity, and gender, Showalter traces the iconography of bodily and mental decay from the writings of doctors and social reformers to its grotesque elaboration in literary fantasy—identifying the syphilitic stigmata not only in the monstrous transformations of *Dracula* or *Dr. Jekyll and Mr. Hyde* but in the perversely wizened features of Hardy's problematic Father Time. Showalter's essay diagnoses both the pervasiveness of this anxious set of signs and the different shapes it assumed in the male and female imaginations. For women, syphilis testified to the horrors of male lust and of female ignorance; for men, to the demon within—but a demon fatally roused by women's rapacity, or goaded to destruction by their coldness. Like others in this volume, Showalter illumines the intersection of literary and sexual politics, and her essay offers a historical sequel to Gallagher's. In the conflict over the meaning of syphilis, Showalter also finds signs of the battle between the sexes in the literary marketplace—a battle ironically intensified by the commercial and aesthetic success of women writers in George Eliot's generation.

In "The Naturalist Machine" Mark Seltzer turns to America to argue that the very form of the naturalist novel served to manage a similar conflict—a competition between rival sexual forces characteristically transformed by the American imagination into a struggle between the Mother and the Machine. The novels of Frank Norris, with their barely concealed terror of the "women people," provide Seltzer an extreme but instructive case; and his sophisticated readings of *The Octopus* and *Vandover and the Brute* locate these works in an anxious discourse about production and generation that ranges from the writings of Thorstein Veblen and Henry Adams to the formulations of nineteenth-century biologists and obstetricians. Seltzer argues that the naturalist novel substituted for the generative power of women and of the earth a "Force" at once abstractly mechanical and imaged as masculine—and thus participated in the systematic technological and masculine takeover of the female body that resulted, for example, in the medicalization of childbirth in the nineteenth century. Reading Norris's novels in terms of the first and second laws of thermodynamics, Seltzer writes of the contradictory way in which generation in naturalist fiction is characteristically associated with a determinist *de*generation—as in Vandover's perverse gestation of, and reversion to, "the Brute." Seltzer contends that the Naturalist Machine reinforces "the power-effects" already inscribed in the realist novel; and his analysis of its operations should thus be read alongside Miller's account of the oblique policing at work in the Novel as Usual.

It is possible, indeed almost conventional, to read "The Beast in the Jungle" as still another narrative about the fear of the female, or at least to understand that John Marcher's true secret is his failure to love May Bartram. But Eve Kosofsky Sedgwick argues that we have been too quick to translate James's obliquities into that familiar moral—and in a daring rereading of the tale in the context of contemporary homosexual panic, she asks what it might mean to recognize that Marcher's unspeakable secret is the "Love that dare not speak its name." Like Showalter and Seltzer, Sedgwick focuses on a moment in Anglo-American history during which anxieties about gender were especially acute; but the fearfully defended boundary to which she draws attention is not that between male and female but the newly created line between the heterosexual and the homosexual. Drawing on recent historians who suggest that "the homosexual" as a separately categorized and fixed person was himself largely an invention of the nineteenth century, Sedgwick explicates the panic that emerged so dramatically toward the century's close as the frightened attempt to distinguish all those bonds between men on which the social order rests from this newly identified form of contamination. By placing John Marcher in the company of the sexually anesthetized heroes in Barrie and Du Maurier and the bitchily domesticated bachelors of Thackeray, Sedgwick offers both a revisionary reading of James and a new character-typology for nineteenth-century fiction. Her provocative essay is a salutary warning about the degree to which a seemingly "universal" reading may conceal a defensive and historically con-ditioned blindness.

The essays in this volume show that criticism of the novel has come a long way from all merely appreciative or celebratory kinds of reading, no matter how subtly refined. Refusing to isolate the writing of fiction from other forms of representation, the authors contribute to an analysis not only of the nineteenth century's novels but of the culture as a whole. The very conver-gence of their arguments in a compelling diagnosis of nineteenth-century anxiety, however—even their success in identifying such anxiety—might prompt us to ask what anxieties of our own this new habit of reading seeks to manage and control. We have been so busy questioning the concealments and evasions of others, especially of our nineteenth-century predecessors, that we may neglect to question our own striking impulse to interrogation. To wonder in turn what energies and obsessions motivate that impulse would be in no sense to diminish the achievement of these essays, but to extend to the present—and to our own practice—the same suspicious alertness that is here so effectively devoted to the writing of the past.

I wish particularly to thank Neil Hertz for his help in editing this volume in the English Institute Series.

RUTH BERNARD YEAZELL
University of California, Los Angeles

SEX, POLITICS, AND SCIENCE
IN THE NINETEENTH-CENTURY NOVEL

D. A. Miller

The Novel as Usual:
Trollope's *Barchester Towers*

—for M. A. and M. B.

I

Where are the police in *Barchester Towers* (1857)? Since they are literally nowhere to be found, the question is bound to seem both insensitive (to what the novel most evidently has chosen to represent) and far too attentive (to what—the evidence is no less compelling—it has not so chosen). The question intrudes as roughly on this novel as might, were they ever to appear in it, the police themselves. So well do the novel's representational and tonal practices avert the question of the police that to a suspicious mind such averting might well amount to an aversion, to a policing of this very question. The suspicion is "paranoid" only if one fails to recognize how difficult it is to give Trollope's fiction, so to speak, another thought: a thought, I mean, that is not wholly determined by the successful operation of the effects of his own novelistic project or that does not simply continue to familiarize us with what is already a highly developed system of familiarizations. In much the same way as one drops into the easy chair that is still the most likely place to read Trollope, or sinks into that half-slumber in which his pages there may be safely skimmed, so one falls into the usual appreciation of his appreciation of the usual, and into the paired assumptions on which it is based: "Life is like this," and "Novels are like this, too." It might require nothing less than impertinence to render as such, and not merely repeat, the terroristic effects of the banality that Trollope, as a matter of principle and program, relentlessly cultivates.

Where, then, are the police in *Barchester Towers*? Though they are literally nowhere to be found, we find them elsewhere, in the exotic space of metaphor. Mr. Slope thrives on the dese-

cration of the Sabbath that he finds useful to lament, "as police-
men do upon the general evil habits of the community," and
Mrs. Proudie calls him to account for his visits to the Signora
Neroni "with the stern look of a detective policeman in the act
of declaring himself."[1] Yet even here, the very archness of the
comparisons advertises an irony that must also prevent us from
taking them entirely seriously. Comically mixing registers,
Trollope reaffirms the decorum that would ordinarily keep
them well separate—at least for anyone except the two ill-
mannered arrivistes who, as he lets us know, are this genteel
novel's male and female devils (241). There may be worse or
simply other aspects to the police than vulgarity, but to give the
devils their due, of all the charges the police metaphor might be
thought to bring against them, this is the only one that is finally
allowed to stick. Blackshirts in the close are an infinitely remote
possibility when, despite his vision of "wheels within wheels"
(136), Slope's extraordinary greasiness is incapable of applying
itself to the social machinery with any effect but the local acts
of mischief that ultimately victimize only him. And by the end
of the novel, even Mrs. Proudie, who after all wears the trousers
only within the patriarchal radius of the strings on her husband's
apron, does "not often" interfere in the arrangement of ecclesiastical affairs in Barchester (504).

In other words, if it is reassuring to know that the police are
only a metaphor in the world of *Barchester Towers,* it is doubly
so to know that this metaphor is also a catachresis, a metaphor
that literally cannot be borne. Not only are there no police in
Barchester Towers, but also—the better to avert the question of
their whereabouts—neither is there anyone who can successfully
assume their function. The ecclesiastical hierarchy of course
supposes just such a function, but at the very top of it, the
bishop, etymologically as well as institutionally charged to
"oversee" his diocese, is quickly reduced to a misnomer. In the
tactics of his wife, his chaplain, and Dr. Grantly, he encounters
three lines of resistance that effectively destroy the coherence

of any personal power of regulation, including that of the tacticians who draw up the lines. And at the bottom of this hierarchy, the churchwardens at Mr. Arabin's new parish are simply "ignorant . . . of the nature of their authority, and of the surveillance which it was their duty to keep" over the vicar himself (204). In any case, there is that about Mr. Arabin which makes even the overbearing archdeacon feel that "it would be difficult to rebuke him with good effect" (458). Characters are scarcely more imposing in the role of what Trollope (in the case of Bertie Stanhope) calls the "social policeman" (405). Cowed by Arabin, Grantly is ready enough to threaten sanctions against Eleanor's presumed treachery with Slope, but—as though to show that the Church militant is no more triumphant in this respect than the Church suffering—when it comes to results, his outraged activism is as null as its opposite: the resigned quietism of Mr. Harding, who refuses even to question his daughter, much less admonish her. All such instances are generalized to the community as a whole at the Ullathorne "fête," where Mr. Plomacy must act "as a sort of head constable as well as master of the revels" (380), and secure the park entrance from intruders. Miss Thorne has already enjoined him not to be "too particular" (340), and her instructions are reinforced when Mr. Greenacre, in the only case of attempted eviction we witness, reminds him not to "stick at trifles" (382). Before the day is half over, even the little work that on such liberal principles remains for him to do is "found to be quite useless": "almost anyone who chose to come made his way into the park" (341).

What is celebrated at Ullathorne is a society that is not only impossible, but unnecessary to police as well. The anarchy that the absence of the police and the failure of their surrogates might commonsensically be assumed to invite is prevented by the autarchy of a world whose own free operation remains in perfect accord with the policing it therefore doesn't require. Something like providence, at work in the most ordinary psychological processes and social interactions, arranges things so that even though everyone goes his or her own way, no one goes astray, and each comes to a place tolerable, if not positively gratifying, to all. Thus, Eleanor and Arabin prove finally as undeserving of the archdeacon's rebukes as she is, and he would be, unmindful of them. And the same ambition that inspires Slope's machinations in Barchester also teaches him to continue them elsewhere, in London, where he marries a sugar-baker's widow. The whole comedy of errors issues in a "rightness" that is all the more impressive for being at once transcendent of any individual design, taken singly, and immanent in all such designs, taken together. When, so to speak, every uninvited plasterer admitted to Ullathorne Park only further cements the social order he finds there, then to negate the police means already to have subsumed them.

The paradox is quite at home in the bourgeois liberal tradition of thought that postulates "freedom" in one dimension (usually inner, spiritual, domestic), the better to accommodate "unfreedom" in another (usually, after the Revolution, social, political, institutional).[2] The absence of the police, together with any need for their controls, would thus seem to imply the familiar double register of middle-class discipline, in which a subject is entitled to freedom only on condition that he or she tactfully internalizes as "self-control" what would otherwise, to achieve the same results, have to appear as massive institutional intervention.[3] Yet what we typically see in Trollope are not repressed characters sternly denying themselves in the interest of the social good that in return guarantees their own well-being, but rather characters who uninhibitedly desire what Trollope calls, in one of his favorite legitimizing phrases, "the good things of the world" (369). (Even Mr. Harding, who rejects these good things in the form of a deanship, appeals to no other ideal than comfort in doing so.) It is strange, therefore—far stranger than the invisible hand of classic bourgeois economics to which the phenomenon bears so strong an analogy—that such characters, severally pursuing a thoroughly worldly happiness, simultaneously contribute to the maintenance of a social order whose cohesiveness and stability make it unique in nineteenth-century fiction. The *sauve-qui-peut* thematics of an individualism run wild, central in a novelist like Balzac, are here as marginal as the police whose absence threatens to engender them. One might dismiss all this as just another element in an almost charmingly naive social fantasmatics, if it did not also more interestingly suggest that social cohesion in Trollope is achieved along other lines of strategy than policial interdictions, whatever their source. Inasmuch as the police are a kind of place-holder for a notion of power as repression, then to grasp with any concreteness how the social field is determined in *Barchester Towers,* where the police literally and finally even metaphorically have no place to hold, we need to rely on a different conception of power that, while it may include policelike restraints, is in no way reducible to them. The police, I said, are negated in *Barchester Towers* only because they have already been subsumed, but what is the nature of that more comprehensive and efficacious polity that, with such few and feeble traces, has absorbed them?

II

The real justice of the peace in *Barchester Towers* is—what might appear to be most in need of one—war itself: not the war that, according to Clausewitz, is the continuation of politics "by other means," but the political power that, according to Foucault and also by other means, is the continuation of war. "If it is true that political power puts an end to war, that it installs, or tries to install, the reign of peace in civil society, this by no means implies that it suspends the effects of war or neutralizes the disequilibrium revealed in the final battle. The role of political power, on this hypothesis, is perpetually to reinscribe this relation through a form of unspoken warfare; to reinscribe it in social institutions, in economic inequalities, in language, in the bodies of each and everyone of us."[4] Barely policed, the social world in Trollope is thoroughly polemicized, and while the impoverished metaphor of the police is capable of yielding only the abstraction of a society that gets along quite well without them, if we only knew how, the abundant metaphor of war pervades and organizes every dimension of the social field. It extends—beyond the "hard battles" fought between the Grantly and Proudie "forces" and the "mutiny in the camp" on either side—from the bedroom politics of Mrs. Proudie and the battle of the sexes implied in every marriage and courtship, to the divided selves of characters as diverse as Slope, Quiverful, and Harding. "War, war, internecine war" (42) is in the archdeacon's heart and—so routinely as to make further evidence merely tedious—in nearly everything else besides.

Yet the metaphor, everywhere present, is everywhere comic as well, as though Trollope were already drawing comfortably on the assurance of social stability that "war," as we will see, works to procure. When the archdeacon liberally celebrates Eleanor's marriage to Arabin, those who know him well understand that his lavish wedding gifts are his hymn of thanksgiving: "He had girded himself with his sword, and gone forth to the war; now he was returning from the field laden with the spoils of the foe. The cob and the cameos, the violoncello and the pianoforte, were all as it were trophies reft from the tent of his now conquered enemy" (504). The vocabulary of final and total victory is hyperbolically out of proportion to a situation in which Slope, like a cat, has fallen on his feet (494), and the cob and the cameos, even if they had been Slope's possessions and not the archdeacon's purchases, make a sorry objective correlative for "spoils." The same overblown quality regularly characterizes a metaphor that, far from establishing the homicidal violence of the Barchester community, reduces it to the innocuous fantasies with which this community (or Trollope speaking on its behalf) seeks to enliven its teapot tempests. Though the bishop might like his wife and Slope to "fight it out so that one

should kill the other utterly, as far as diocesan life was concerned" (234), he knows as well as we do that this is wishful
thinking. The mock-heroics of the war metaphor turn war into a
war game, so diminished in its aspirations and consequences that
no one sustains serious bodily harm (even the devils: Mrs. Proudie
is merely tripped up, and Slope is only he who gets slapped) or
serious harm of any kind. On the contrary, in the course of the
long theological polemic conducted between Slope and Arabin,
"each had repeatedly hung the other on the horns of a dilemma;
but neither seemed to be a whit the worse for the hanging; and
so the war went on merrily" (116). Perhaps one reason it can do
so is that the "final battle," in which the essential power relations of society would be decided, has already and long ago taken
place, with the conclusion of a sanguinary religious politics in
England at the end of the seventeenth century. Like, in a different national history, Stendhal's "Restoration comedy," Trollope's merry war exists as a belated copy, petty and peaceable,
of a belligerent and heroic original—with the difference of course
that modern bloodlessness appears in Trollope's color scheme
less black than rose. Thus seeming to retract its very tenor, the
war metaphor would be as catachretic as that of the police, were
it not for the fact that, while there does not appear to be much
policing in *Barchester Towers,* there is a great deal of fighting.
Accordingly, since it is a question of "war by other means," its
displacement and reinscription, one cannot rest entirely assured
that the war metaphor functions only to self-destruct: as though
it could also be taken for granted that political struggles always
bore world-historical freight; that social conflict, when it had
ceased to deal death, did not continue to administer life; and
that mere war games were incapable of inciting power plays.

"What is the use," then, we ask with Mrs. Grantly, "of always
fighting?" (456). Her question is rhetorical not because there is
no use, as she seems to think, but because—at least for the novel's
major instance of fighting—Trollope has already answered it:
"We are much too apt to look at schism in our church as an

unmitigated evil. Moderate schism, if there may be such a thing, at any rate calls attention to the subject, draws in supporters who would otherwise have been inattentive to the matter, and teaches men to think upon religion" (169–70). This "moderate schism" in fact structures both the clerical infighting in *Barchester Towers* and the considerable institutional and social coherence accruing to it. "If there may be such a thing"? There can scarcely be anything else in the novel, where schism reaches neither the rupture nor the healing that are, alternatively, its promised ends. War is total inasmuch as victory never is. The controversies and power struggles that seem to throw such dishonor on the Church are not likely ever to be resolved, and only an outsider and parvenu like Slope is naive enough to harbor "a view to putting an end to schism in the diocese" (305). The rest, including the dominant Grantlyites, are practically willing to abide in that interminable state of compromise which is always part victory, part defeat. Yet as Franco Moretti has seen, the distinctive function of compromise is not " 'to make everybody happy' "–or even, for that matter, to make anybody happy—but rather "to create a broad area with uncertain boundaries where polarized values come into contact, cohabit, become hard to recognize and disentangle."[5] Similarly, the "use" of fighting in *Barchester Towers* is not to resolve once for all the issues at hand, but to bind the combatants to the capacious institution that sponsors their disputes. To contend over introducing Sabbath-day schools, or intoning the Sunday service, is not just to advertise the supreme importance of the Church of England in the national life. Even better, it is to make this importance vital in the contending subjects themselves, whose conflicts (amounting to so many cathexes) attach them not only to "religion" but also to the general social condition of bondedness that not inaptly passes here under that name. The entelechy of a war game, therefore, is not, as with a war, to be over, but, as with a game, to secure a maximum of play. What matters most in this game is not whether you win or lose, or even how well you play it, but that you play it at all.

We begin to see why Trollope's fiction frequently turns on contemporary social, political, and legal "issues," but also why it is at the same time so relatively indifferent to their substance, and so little eager to take sides. Rarely more developed than Hitchcock's "Macguffin," the issues are at bottom only pretexts to mobilize the novelistic population for a merry war. Trollope inflects the "social problem novel" so that any "problem" is already part of a more fundamental social solution: namely, the militant constitution and operation of the social field as such. Thus, on one hand, *Barchester Towers* may be thought to be about the Oxford Movement, insofar as the latter provides a referential matrix for the controversies and struggles that the novel represents. Yet on another, *Barchester Towers* is only "about" the Oxford Movement in the sense of skirting around it. This is not a novel from which one hopes—for which one even needs—to learn much about the movement, except perhaps the somewhat cynical knowledge that very little finally was moved by it. The movement makes a strictly token appearance here: in the references to items like roods, waistcoats, and so forth, which—deprived of any theological rationale—seem merely partisan badges or personal tics. Just as he will later (in the Palliser novels) portray a Parliament that, for all its politicking, has no politics, so here Trollope creates a Church without elaborating its theology. Indicatively, the volumes of this theology in the cathedral library are "not disturbed, perhaps, quite as often as from the appearance of the building the outside public might have been led to expect" (168), and though the polemic between Arabin and Slope is said to concern the apostolic succession, what either has to urge on the matter is never reported. In the formalism of power to which Trollope reduces his Church, theology comes down to an ad hoc allusion or two, as though only in the most perfunctory fashion to motivate the device that is thereby laid bare.

The intellectual dearth of an explicit set of ideas about God, man, revelation, and so on, is more than matched by the affective absence of anything like spiritual intensity. We have only to think of the rendering of religious feeling in George Eliot, where major characters are compulsively and hysterically overcome by it, to appreciate how levelheadedly secular Trollope's priests and "priestesses" are. Eliot's kind of urgency has no place in this novel, and though Bertie Stanhope's many and silly conversions do, Arabin must already have passed through his more serious religious crisis before he is allowed entry, and then only to learn that "the greatest mistake any man ever made is to suppose that the good things of the world are not worth the winning" (369–70). The point that clergymen are no better than other men is fondly and repeatedly made: the archdeacon calculates his chances of a bishopric at his father's deathbed; Slope succumbs to a passion for a married signora; Dr. Stanhope idles in Italy; and Tom Staple drinks. As in the notable conversation over Sunday lunch at the Thornes, which admixes with "all manner of ecclesiastical subjects" generous amounts of guano (211–12), the sacred has only to put forth its claim and—like any other pretension in comedy—it is brought down to earth.

Barchester Towers thus doubly demystifies the institution-as-religion, which not only lacks a higher agenda than the need (via moderate schism) to maintain itself but is also manned by a very ordinary run of men. In either case, institutional power is portrayed quite apart from an official account of its workings. The ostensive issues that such power engages are revealed in all their inconsequence as merely the means to secure institutional consolidation, ramification, and tenure. And the agents of such power come quickly to be divested of the halo that those to whom they minister—or whom they administer—wrongly but not unnaturally suppose them to wear. Reducing religion to an institution like any other, the novel achieves a compelling insight into the typical ideological process that is thus reversed: the self-promotion of an institution to the status of religion. One might applaud the insight, were it not the basis for endorsing the very phenomenon it uncovers, and for comfortably transferring all the authority of religion to the social-institutional domain. Mr. Arabin, the novel's "intellectual," tells Eleanor:

> Our contentions do bring on us some scandal. The outer world, though it constantly reviles us for our human infirmities, and throws in our teeth the fact that being clergymen we are still no more than men, demands of us that we should do our work with godlike perfection. There is nothing godlike about us: we differ from each other with the acerbity common to man—we triumph over each other with human frailty—we allow differences on subjects of divine origin to produce among us antipathies and enmities which are anything but divine. This is all true. But what would you have in place of it? There is no infallible head for a church on earth. This dream of believing man has been tried, and we see in Italy and in Spain what has come of it. Grant that there are and have been no bickerings within the pale of the Pope's Church. Such an assumption would be utterly untrue; but let us grant it, and then let us say which church has incurred the heavier scandals. (195)

Much as, in late-twentieth-century America, unseemly political activity against imperialist wars or for various civil rights is opportunistically converted into the very evidence of the "free society" that this activity is in fact trying to bring about, or a scandal like Watergate comes to vindicate a system that, even so severely tried, still triumphantly "works," so the bickering in Trollope's Church and the fallibility of its ministers are all to the good. They confer on this Church its liberal Anglican identity, in contradistinction to the authoritarian Church of Rome. More than a simple mechanism or function, "moderate schism" is a supreme value and one whose religious implications easily gradate into political and social ones. With his comparisons to Italy and Spain, Arabin might almost be referring to the merits of a bicameral legislature or a two-party system (as Prime Minister Palliser actually will), or even to economic productivity. It is no less clear in the case of the all-too-human clergy that Trollope's disabused treatment of religion is only a subtler means of valorizing the social order that religion serves. Fond as he is of showing that clergymen are no more than men, Trollope is even fonder of showing that most of them, at any rate, are no less than gentlemen, with the civility and tolerance of such. The clergy are not debunked so much as brought under a wider and more generous set of social norms, as though religion itself were the old dispensation and "the social" the new. These norms— the novel's truly operative ethical criteria—still condemn Slope's advances to the signora (though as more inept than immoral), but they perfectly accommodate Dr. Gwynne's gout.

Necessarily, then, the demystifications stop short of impugning the category of the sacred from which the Church draws its institutional authority, for it is a matter of broadening this authority, not blasting it. "I may question the infallibility of the teachers, but I hope that I shall not therefore be accused of doubt as to the thing taught" (45). This is sufficiently pious to allow the demystifications to proceed without scandal even to the legendarily proper sensibilities of the middle-class mid-Victorian reader, who does not seem to have protested that "the thing to be taught" is as little specified as the teachers' doctrinal disputes (which do, however, necessarily shadow it in "doubt"). Abstractly upholding the claims of religion, the novelist's disclaimer promotes their concrete secularization: doctrinally vacant, Trollope's piety amounts to no more—but also to no less—than throwing a general transcendent aura over socially current norms of decent behavior. Similarly, his occasional but conspicuous gesture of blanking out the sacred from the novel has a double valence. At the same time that it piously retains the "prestige" of the sacred, it slyly neutralizes any otherness that might prevent the sacred from being assimilated to the way we live now. "It would not be becoming were I to travestie a sermon, or even to repeat the language of it in the pages of a novel" (45). It is a moot point whether what inspires the censorship here is a religious injunction, as against graven images (of which the printed fiction one calls a novel would be the most recent example), or a social protocol that determines the norm of what is or is not "becoming." In the very act of separating the sacred from the profane, the two are only further entangled.

In Trollope sometimes to omit the sacred in its orthodox form is—not least by this very means—always to include it as the social order itself.

To this one must add that if religion is thus diffused as social schismatics, then diffused along with it is a certain structure of hegemony. Certainly, Arabin's theory of moderate schism, echoing and elaborating Trollope's own, implies the necessity of pluralism, dialogue, the universal embrace of various divergent views even as one militates for one such view in particular. Yet it also matters that it is Arabin who advances this theory, which therefore issues from the ideological wing of the party most "in power." Consider this pair of contrasts. Mr. Slope means "to rule without terms" (237), "conceives it to be his duty to know all the private doings and desires of the flock entrusted to his care" (28), and finds it expedient "that there should be but one opinion among the dignitaries of the diocese" (305). But as long as those around Dr. Grantly "fully and freely admitted the efficacy of Mother Church, [the archdeacon] was willing that that mother should be merciful and affectionate, prone to indulgence, and unwilling to chastize" (27): "He liked to give laws and be obeyed in them implicitly, but he endeavoured that his ordinances should be within the compass of the man, and not unpalatable to the gentleman" (28). And again: While Mrs. Proudie, "habitually authoritative to all," "stretches her power over all [her husband's] movements, and will not even abstain from things spiritual," Mrs. Grantly "values power, and has not unsuccessfully striven to acquire it; but she knows what should be the limits of a woman's rule" (20). The case for pluralism, or for the separation and distribution of powers, is never made by the outsiders, who might seem to secure themselves a hearing thereby, but who are instead—in a familiar pattern that extends far beyond Barchester—characterized as shrilly authoritarian. It may only be a measure of the constraint implied in the system of liberal tolerance that the characterization, also as usual, is all too plausible. For what Slope and Mrs. Proudie implicitly contest

is, more than mere "positions," the very ground on which positions may be contested (or at least, this is how it must always
appear when such ground virtually coincides with the "high and
dry Church" party that occupies it). His demand for "but one
opinion" in the diocese rejects the very principle that makes the
game possible, just as her will to participate in what is strictly a
man's game represents an unthinkable change in the rules. They
are therefore defeated not *in* so much as *by* the game, which is
too well entrenched not to be played in any case, even when
players refuse to cooperate. Dissenting from the game itself,
Slope is made to speak a fascist discourse that only further dis-
credits his play in it. And if in the end Mrs. Proudie fares better
than the self-exiled Slope, this is only because she is saved by
the inconsistency that is, Trollope would tell us, a woman's
privilege. In practice she must be more tolerant—more submis-
sive to the limits of a woman's rule—than her evident intentions
ever quite recognize: the same patriarchy that makes outrages
like hers inevitable also makes their consequences minimal.
While the outsiders, then, talk a totalitarianism that, to the
extent an attempt is made to practice as well as preach it, only
keeps them outside, insiders like Arabin and Grantly eloquently
defend and practically cultivate a pluralism that stands thus
revealed as not just a mechanism of social consolidation but also
and coincidentally an ideology of social dominance. What matters
most about the war game is that it continue to be played, since
it is the game itself that most fundamentally ensures partisan
privileges and social imbalances. Small wonder, then, that at
Oxford Arabin "talked jovially over his glass of port of the ruin
to be anticipated by the Church, and of the sacrilege committed
daily by the Whigs" (173): the merry war is not a free-for-all.

III

The formal name for "moderate schism" would no doubt be
plot—except that moderate schism, even extended to include all
instances of fighting in *Barchester Towers*—does not quite

amount to what ordinarily grips us under that term. It is odd that a narrative declaring itself "war" should be so open to charges of blandness. The frequent observation that "nothing happens" in Trollope, absurd if one is counting up narrative incidents, is true enough in the sense that these incidents occur in the absence of that strong teleology which, elsewhere in Victorian fiction, would allow them to gain point (as major climax or minor anticipation, in the beginning, middle, or end). Geared primarily to its own self-sustenance, moderate schism is useless in calling a halt—or even giving much direction—to the narrative, which as a result seems underplotted: more a meandering succession of episodes than a dynamic progression en route to Aristotelian catharsis or Freudian working-through. It is not that a novel like *Barchester Towers* quite deserves to be called "open-ended," though like very few nineteenth-century English novels, it both has and is a sequel. But even as the traditional closural chords are touched (the settlement of the good, the banishment or silencing of the bad), Trollope offers them as little more than expedients in the business of turning out products for the novel market. The end of a saleable novel, like the end of a children's party, requires such "sweetmeats and sugar-plums" (502). When the text commodifies itself at such points, moreover, the item for sale is surely not just closure but its ironical negation as well. In any case, market considerations are not confined to determining Trollope's archly conventional closures. They determine none the less those loose and casual plots whose refusal to elaborate structures of secrecy or suspense is, in the Victorian context, the least conventional aspect of his fiction. For while a strong sense of an ending may get the novels sold, it is a weak sense of one—the condition for Trollope's unequalled productivity among his contemporaries—that gets them written in lucrative quantities. Like a builder working under a slack construction code, Trollope may erect the houses of his fiction rapidly and all over the tract. Yet the evident cynicism of the artist-as-entrepreneur is rehabilitated in the happy marriage of convenience, celebrated throughout Trollope's work, between the Novel and the social order that (in more than one way) it represents. What at the phase of novel production is the superior efficiency of relaxing teleological construction (the endings are now detachable parts, for swifter assembly) shows up in the finished novel-product as the viability of a social order that, bound together in perennial militancy, no more foresees a resolution to the "problems" that in fact sustain it than it envisions its own coming-to-an-end. If closure does not carry much conviction in Trollope, neither does it need to: the social security that traditional closure means to establish has been displaced into the tensions, differences, and disequilibriums that engender or motivate the narrative processes themselves.

"But the novelist has other aims than the elucidation of his plot," and the sheer readiness with which Trollope, in his own public relations, concedes his imperfections in this branch of work notifies us that he bases his claims to our attention elsewhere. "The novelist has other aims than the elucidation of his plot. He desires to make his readers so intimately acquainted with his characters that the creations of his brain should be to them speaking, moving, living, human creatures. . . .–And as, here in our outer world, we know that men and women change,– become worse or better as temptation or conscience may guide them,–so should these creations of his change, and every change should be noted by him. . . . If the would-be novelist have aptitudes that way, all this will come to him without much struggling;–but if it do not come, I think he can only make novels of wood."[6] Rather in the way that a given sociopolitical issue provides only a pretext to set the plot going, so it is implied that plot itself need be no more than a makeshift for the primordial exhibition of character. Plot seems to exhaust its only valid function in foregrounding, along with certain general truths about human nature, certain specific truths about its varieties, inasmuch as these are the real burden of representation. Concomitantly, the motivations of plot (in social schismatics) tend to be all but dismissed as so many local or contingent occasions permitting the display of such truths. The priority that Trollope accords the category of character thus belongs to the "depoliticizing" ambition of his fiction, like the indifference of this fiction to the polemics that it at once excites and refuses to be excited by. As, formally speaking, character takes precedence over plot, which merely affords an opportunity for rendering it, so, in a thematic dimension, the human agent stands above the social fray to which he or she can never be reduced.

Yet even as Trollope foregoes the elaboration of plot for the exposition of character, he hardly thereby remits the problematics of merry warfare, which are rather displaced into the constitution of the subject who wages it. For what does the well-advertised complexity of his characters come to if not the simple effect, almost gimmicky in its insistence, of showing that they have "mixed motives"? Trollopean man, like Trollopean woman, is every bit as much a "moderate schism" as the social disputes in which he contends. Thus, the archdeacon, committed to upholding the Church, likes to broadcast his enjoyment of "the good things of this world" (27). Arabin loves Eleanor, but as he also knows, he loves her money too (323). Mr. Quiverful is anxious for means to quiet his butcher, but equally anxious to be right with his own conscience (218). "In his indecision, his weakness, his proneness to be led by others," Mr. Harding— who on occasion, however, can show resolution enough—is "very far from being perfect" (154). An unsexed virago whose milk has been exchanged for a not entirely Shakespearean gall, Mrs. Proudie proves herself so far a woman as to be "touched" by Mrs. Quiverful's unquiet desperation (241). And so on. Even Mr. Slope is not in all things a bad man: "His motives, like those of most men, were mixed, and though his conduct was generally very different from that which we would wish to praise, it was actuated perhaps as often as that of the majority of the world by a desire to do his duty" (123). Characters are at war within themselves no less than they are at war with one another, and the implied politics of subjectivity are both isomorphic and continuous with the politics of the social that, as we will see, they underwrite. Tellingly, it is the fascist Slope who is most willing to rationalize himself into pure, single-minded will, as though the despot's first conquest were of necessity over himself. "He had early in life devoted himself to works which were not compatible with the ordinary pleasures of youth, and he had abandoned such pleasures not without a struggle" (124). If what undoes Slope politically is his refusal to recognize an already and solidly constituted party system, what undoes him psychologically is his repression of the passional drives that, willy-nilly, return to humiliate even his own sense of ethics. Sex in this guardian of morality has been buried alive, and its reemergence from the vault is correspondingly violent. "Mr. Slope tried hard within himself to cast off the pollution with which he felt that he was defiling his soul" (254), but insofar as to cast off or emit a pollution is precisely what pollution entails, the energy of resistance is already the compulsiveness of surrender: "He could not help himself. Passion, for the first time in his life, passion was too strong for him" (245-46). By contrast, Arabin, whose "weakness" it has ever been "to look for impure motives for his own conduct" (323), sits far more comfortably in his skin. Personality begins to resemble a parliamentary democracy, appertaining to multiple constituencies, and any attempt to deny this structure—which in this version appears no less than ontologically grounded—seems only to confirm its existence to the discomfort of the usurping member. Like the war game that always wins, most of all when it is the game itself that is being contested, so the heterogeneity of the subject invariably triumphs over every effort to purify it.

There is—or would be, if Trollope ever went to extremes—a paradox in his conception of character, in the sense that precisely what is alleged to make character interesting—its variability—also risks undermining the coherence that allows character to flourish as a valid category in the first place. What besides a proper name could hold the self together once it were radically split into discontinuities? Yet for all the shades of difference within the characters in *Barchester Towers*, what they shade is an eminently recognizable unit of self-identity: a totality that compels into integration the parts that thereby "compose" it. It is as though each character were governed by a principle of majority rule that both necessitates diversity and simultaneously dominates it. Like the moderate schism of Trollope's sociology, the moderate schizophrenia of his psychology organizes divergent motives according to an ethical dominant—as it were, a moral majority—that in the last analysis (and therefore even in the first) determines their play. This dominant founds a character's coherence and continues to subject him or her to the moral judgments that Trollope, like most of his fellow Victorian novelists, has no wish to abandon. (If his judgments are more nuanced than is usual in Victorian fiction, it is because they too are structured around a dominant that imposes itself through its willingness to "tolerate" that which it dominates.) Thus, for all his mixed motives, Slope remains fundamentally repellent, and despite his imperfections, Harding generally wins our admiration. The archdeacon, a more complicated instance, may dare to ask himself whether he covets a bishopric whose price is his father's life, but: "the question was answered in a moment. The proud, wishful, worldly man, sank on his knees by the bedside, and taking the bishop's hand within his own, prayed eagerly that his sins might be forgiven him" (3-4). It does not much matter that no sooner has the father died than the son angles to succeed him in the palace, for the essential moral demonstration— the worldling draws the line at selling his soul—has been made. The parliamentary structure of personality thus "calls for a division" in a double sense: the same organization that allows all disputants to speak also periodically compels them to vote, and thus to determine which party holds sway.

We are now in a position to address a key question that the notion of moderate schism inevitably raises—namely, what keeps it moderate? What prevents the differences of opinion and sentiment that constitute the social field from reaching an intensity at which they constitute a threat to it? It will be recalled from *The Warden* (1855) that one of the founding gestures of Trollope's work is the derision it casts on the precursive achievement of Dickens—a derision that specifically targets the Dickensian forms of institution and character. In "The Almshouse," by Mr. Popular Sentiment, an absurdly one-dimensional institution given over to pure exploitation recruits exploiters and exploited alike from a population of absurdly one-dimensional human subjects. The carceral uniformity of the institution entails the impermeability of the subject (or vice versa) as a container of undiluted good or evil. Trollope's real rejoinder to Dickens, however, comes in the oeuvre that goes beyond satire to offer its own alternative treatment of the same concerns. The institutional landscape, for instance, is no more pervasive in Dickens than in Trollope, who is in fact the only Victorian novelist to rival him in the amount of attention he pays to institutional phenomena (not just the Church and Parliament, but also the school, the civil service, the law). This landscape is, in fact, ubiquitous in Trollope, where there is no place—like home in Dickens—to retreat from it. It is as though Trollope had liberated from its characteristic Dickensian confinement the institution, which is consequently at large to traverse and structure the entire social field. Yet if flight is now impossible, neither is there the same need to flee, since what is stifling about institutions in Dickens is aerated in Trollope's representation of them. No longer the melodramatically closed site of a monolithic and homogeneous oppression, the institution has become—no doubt, more plausibly—a wide, highly variegated network, with multiple and mutually correcting jurisdictions. Thus, in *Barchester Towers,* if the bishop may appoint the warden of Hiram's Hospital, it is the archdeacon who is entitled to fill the living at St. Ewold's, and neither has any authority to select the dean. And just as the dean and chapter have the right to exclude Slope from the cathedral pulpit, so Harding may resign the

wardenship or refuse the deanship. Dickens's insight into the
institution-as-confinement induces a claustrophobia so exas-
perating that the only proper political response to it seems to be
"a direct attack on the whole system,"[7] but in Trollope's vision of
the institution-as-"schism," resistance follows the usual bureaucratic instructions to apply elsewhere, in another department.
Mediated by numerous overlapping and realigning divisions of
power, social warfare is kept from lapsing into a single and sustained binary opposition, or from aggregating the intensities
that drive it forward into mass movements. Not only are there
always more than two sides in this war; they are reapportioned
in every skirmish as well.

The system is further complicated—moderated—by being
anchored in a subject whose own internal schismatics likewise
atomize the intensities they generate. The "sides" of war are
thus doubly distributed: between different subjects across an
imbricated social-institutional surface, and within the same
subject, who is simultaneously attached to more than one point
on this surface. By virtue of one set of commitments, for example, Harding belongs to the Grantlyite party, but through
another, he does not hate the chaplain as the archdeacon does
(154) and so countenances Slope's courtship of Eleanor. Similarly, though Slope sees at once the necessity of "open battle
against Dr. Grantly and all Dr. Grantly's adherents" (43), he
also develops an interest in Dr. Grantly's sister-in-law, which he
tries to promote by getting her father the wardenship, even at
the risk of alienating his only ally, Mrs. Proudie. His sexuality,
moreover, compelling him to the side of Signora Neroni's couch,
undermines all these projects, much as a certain loyalty to her
sex ultimately tempers the Signora's own designs on Arabin. All
in all, the political commotion occasioned by Bishop Grantly's
demise seems scarcely less fortuitous as it develops than the tim-
ing of his death. Trollope is positively eager to feature a politics
that stems not from meditated strategy (or even from the dialectic
that will always have its reasons), but from the happenstance

and "comic" conjunction of events, persons, motives belonging to radically different series. In the matter of the wardenship, Slope finds himself working to realize the desires of his enemy, and in the case of the deanship, whatever Grantly thinks, "not he, but circumstances, had trampled on Mr. Slope" (497). Yet if politics is thus conspicuously devoid of the coherence that its self-appointed directors have planned, it does not lack coherence of another kind. Whether the subject is the effect of the social schismatics he or she "internalizes," or whether these schismatics are the collective "projection" of a psychological structure, in either case, the continuity between the social order and the subject who relays it makes for a supremely steady State, un-staggered by the militancy that, in the very act of diffusing, they collaborate to defuse.

IV

The subsumption of religion under the social alerts us to the novel's own inherence in the latter category, which alone entitles (and is entitled to) representation. It may not be becoming to repeat the language of a sermon in the pages of a novel, but it is taken for granted that the novel has a right to rehearse the social interactions that have traditionally been the proper object of its imitation of life. Yet the system Trollope calls moderate schism is not just a fact about the social world that he elects to describe; nor is it even just a fact about the social world that he does his best to valorize. Far more immediately and concretely than either its representation as theme or its designation as value, the system operates in the novel's own representational technol-ogy and in the reading practice that this determines. As we will see, it is too simple to say that Trollopean narration merely doubles thematic structures with its own more or less analo-gous forms. But even if this were all it did, it would always be doing more than this, in positing as an incontestable readerly "experience" the ideological propositions that, even when eventually stated as such, have therefore already won a fundamental assent. The spiritual exercise of reading the novel catches us in confirming that which we might wish to bring into question, even before we quite know what this involves. Accordingly, whatever dissent we do manage is likely to remain within the bounds of moderation, since we have already put into practice some of the basic tenets of what gets preached. At best, a character like Arabin, even when he is being used as the novelist's mouthpiece, can only make a virtue of necessity, throwing a system that operates in any case into the flattering half-light of ideology. But the novelist can go him one better and make a necessity of virtue, embedding his political values in a specific course of formal operations to which any reader of his novel, including the most hostile, is inevitably subject. Perhaps the best instance of how technique drills us in doctrine concerns the virtue that is the very ethos of moderate schism, a virtue that is quite simply impossible to read Trollope without exercising: tolerance.

In the warring world of *Barchester Towers,* tolerance is the moral consciousness that allows partisans to transcend the one-sided particularity of their cause. Through tolerance, characters acknowledge and uphold the general polity that submits their aims to varying degrees of compromise and even counterfinality. That the winners in the merry war are notably more tolerant than the losers no doubt owes something to the sentimental Victorian stipulation that only the meek shall inherit the earth; but it owes more, we have seen, to the hegemonic structure that is to be tolerated. One might even point to the practical advantages that tolerance—as the foundation of a *Realpolitik*—gives in maneuvering. "It will be unseemly of us to show ourselves in a bad humour," advises Dr. Gwynne after the bishop's appointment of Quiverful; "moreover, we have no power in this matter, and it will therefore be bad policy to act as though we had" (420). Having minorized his power here, however, Gwynne is able to exercise it the more successfully later on, when he is instrumental not only in "representing in high places the claims which Mr. Harding had upon the Government," but also in "getting the offer [of the deanship] transferred to Mr. Arabin" (495). Yet tolerance, though always an objective state of affairs in Barchester, is not often a subjective state of mind among the Barchester warriors—for the good reason that, were it wholly to engross consciousness, it might undermine the beliefs that must remain sufficiently unsuspended to be worth fighting for. Combatants must know they are right, and such conviction as militancy requires easily blinds them to the irreducibility of other "sides." Conversely, insofar as a tolerant appreciation of these other sides tends to relativize beliefs into the mere system of differences that makes a game possible, then the players of such a game cannot be counted on to be quite so hard at play. Psychologically speaking, too much tolerance is as debilitating in the merry war as too little, and the intolerant Slope no more misses his mark than the all-too-tolerant Bertie Stanhope, whose halfhearted schemes are plagued with futility from the outset. Arabin and Grantly are careful to promote tolerance only before a battle has begun, or after it is over, or during a lull in the hostilities. Less careful, the unceasingly tolerant Harding is so unfit for war that his weakness takes the socially alarming form of a refusal to fight at all. The same social engineering that makes tolerance an indispensable formal condition of moderate schism also makes it equally indispensable that the schismatizers largely "forget" this fact.

The narration, however, embodies the tolerant consciousness more amply and consistently than the characters ever can. One notices, for instance, that Trollope's prescriptions for the sympathetic depiction of characters as "living, human creatures," are somewhat belied by the evenhanded detachment of his actual treatment of them. At whatever point the novelist must learn to hate his characters and to love them, "must argue with them, quarrel with them, forgive them, and even submit to them,"[8]

by the time of composition he has also evidently learned to
moderate the degree of his affective involvement in them. At
the heart of our reading of most other Victorian fiction lies an
affective schema as adolescent as the protagonists who command
our attention therein: those whom we love struggle with those
whom we hate, against a background of those to whom we are
largely indifferent. The schema is grounded, of course, in the
imaginary, specular relationship that the novelist's own partiality encourages us to form with one character in particular—
usually the one we call the hero. This primary identification
determines a host of secondary ones—with the hero's allies,
against the hero's enemies—in what amounts overall to an exclusive and hierarchical organization of affect. The jubilation of
my identification with David Copperfield, for example, entails
my unequivocal acceptance of Peggotty, the nice variations in
my response to Betsey Trotwood and Steerforth, my amused
lack of concern for the Micawbers, and my peremptory rejection
of the Murdstones. Even George Eliot's programmatic attempt
to compensate for the effects of this single (or singularly intense)
emotional focus is not quite the same thing as abandoning it,
and her narrator's periodic gesturing to, say, Casaubon's point
of view only succeeds in reinforcing our initial sympathy for
Dorothea's—as though the decisive proof of Casaubon's repul-
siveness were that he remained chilling even after benefit of so
remarkably generous an apology. One might almost make the
case that the high or simply Philistine moral insistence of most
Victorian novels exonerates what is in fact a kind of emotional
bigotry. Trollope, however, plays so fair in this regard that he
can freely admit to liking one character (like Eleanor) and dis-
liking another (such as Slope), as novelists who play favorites
never do. This is primarily a matter of limiting, in both extent
and depth, the affective intensity that his narration brings to
focus on a character. On the one hand, it would be difficult
even to identify, much less identify with, the "hero" of *Barchester Towers*, so evenly and dispassionately does the novelist's

shifting attention circulate among all his characters. And on the other, even when his preferences are declared, they never impede a cool and constant appraisal of imperfections, so that no great discrepancy in either tone or treatment separates likable characters from unlikable ones. For all of Trollope's emphasis on rendering a character in the fulness of his or her particularity, it is from an enmiring attachment to this particularity that Trollopean narration regularly takes flight. Instead of loving this character and hating that one, Trollope is at once charmed and irritated by them all, thus cultivating a pluralistic appreciation of the value—as well as the limitations—that each in one context or another proves to have. In contradistinction to George Eliot, Charlotte Brontë, or Dickens, whose sometimes ruthless emotional simplifications are but one step removed (what reader has not taken the step?) from a Stalinist wish that large segments of the novelistic population be purged, Trollope gives structure to an accommodating perception that it truly takes all kinds to make a world.

What facilitates the affective detachment from characters, however, is the novelist's minute and sustained moral appraisal of them, from which none escapes in any condition to be the object of an idealizing overinvestment. The very excuses made for characters are often the best evidence of the accusations implied against them. "Our archdeacon was worldly—who among us is not so?" (9). Yet were we all so, the worldliness would scarcely be worth observing in the first place, or the observation worth repeating on almost every occasion the archdeacon appears. Eleanor's "devotion to her late husband was fast fading" under the pressure of Arabin and Bertie Stanhope: "Will anyone blame my heroine for this?" (214, 215). Perhaps no one would, but for the blame that the exoneration presupposes. Poverty had had an effect on Mr. Quiverful "not beneficial either to his spirit, or his keen sense of honour": "Who can boast that he would have supported such a burden with a different result?" (217–18). All the same, the fact that we might have behaved similarly never shakes our conviction that Quiverful's spirit is as tremulous as his sense of honor is dull. Trollope's tolerance thus includes an acute consciousness of all that needs to be tolerated. It requires—or better, requisitions—the stuff on which to exercise itself, and this involves, in addition to the humane impulse to understand, mitigate, and accept shortcomings, a less evident commitment to finding them out. Trollope's generosity toward his characters regularly depends on what ought to be equally notorious: his carping attention to even their least moral failings, which he never ceases to hold in view. The paradox of his tolerance is that it is willing to overlook only that which it has closely looked over: it accepts "regardless" what in fact has been put under careful and critical scrutiny. It is thus a mild manner of promoting such scrutiny, as though subjects could be brought all the more frequently before a tribunal whose sentences are so lenient. Like the clergymen, the novelist of *Barchester Towers* has his own cure of souls: that congregation of characters whose little vagrancies he untiringly tracks down in his concern for the welfare of each and all. In fact, Slope's wish "to know all the private doings and desires of the flock entrusted to his care" (28) would be far better satisfied in the position of the omniscient Victorian novelist, who must know whether his charges be true or false, "and how far true, and how far false."[9] And Slope's reflections on the superiority of "spiritual" over "temporal" modalities of power are no less pertinent to the novelist than to the priest whose pastorate the novelist appears in any case to have largely taken over: "The temporal king, judge, or gaoler can work but on the body. The spiritual master, if he have the necessary gifts and can duly use them, has a wider field of empire. He works upon the soul. If he can make himself be believed, he can be all powerful over those who listen" (27). From this perspective, all that distinguishes Slope's ambition from Trollope's practice—though it quite suffices to scapegoat the chaplain as a monster of intolerance—is the end to which pastoral power is solicited. Inasmuch as Slope aims to impose "but one opinion" on the diocese, such knowledge of differences as he is intent on acquiring would support a program of repressing them. Repression, however, is just what Trollope's nice account of the number, degree, and extent of his characters' weaknesses stops short of inviting. His tolerance follows fascism up to the point of martialing the data for a case that, departing from fascism, it never prosecutes. Instead, it dissipates its findings by assimilating individual delinquencies to the general ways of humankind: "which of us has not . . . ?" We would call this generosity, as many have done, if it did not always underline how much was owing to it—or if, far from effacing the normative grid that determines delinquencies, it did not extend the grid all the way to "us" and our own self-perception. Thus, if the easygoing Trollope foregoes some of his customary aplomb in presenting Slope, he needs to surrender almost as much when it comes to introducing the Stanhopes, who represent an opposite, but complementary, threat to tolerance. Whereas Slope refuses to accept differences, the Stanhopes tend not even to recognize them, mainly or altogether ignoring the value-discriminations in which tolerance finds its footing. Of course, what Trollope rebukes most sharply in this clerical family is the want of religious principle. The father manifests no belief in the Church he laxly serves; the daughters are the one "a pure free-thinker" (66) and the other a devotee of "latitudinarian philosophy" (70); and the son flirts indifferently with Jesuits and Jews. But to the extent that "religion" merely names the transcendent status conferred on community bonding and on "becoming" norms of conduct, it is the social atheism of the Stanhopes that is the real target of censure. Though "they bore and forebore" (64), there is no basis in conviction, value, or norm from which forebearance proceeds. Bertie's indifference to religion, for example, extends pointedly to value-criteria of any kind, whether moral ("no virtue could charm him, no vice shock him"), social ("he had no respect for rank, and no aversion to those below him"), economic (the "prudence" of the scheme to catch Eleanor is "antagonistic to his feelings"), or even aesthetic (his art gravitates naturally toward the carnivalesque genre of caricature). "All people were nearly alike to him. He was above, or rather below, all prejudices" (73-74). What will finally require his family's departure from Barchester (only shortly before Slope's) is precisely their inferiority to those "prejudices" which tolerance not only works by invoking but also, in the process, works to invoke.

If tolerance is thus a mode of normalization, normalization is equally a mode of tolerance. For the norms "secreted" in Trollope's narration (as gradually as secretions, as inferentially as secrets) are not concerned to determine behavior as such, which is on the contrary avidly gathered under them in all its variety. What these norms do determine, however, is our consciousness of behavior, and whatever diversity appears in the characters' lives never exceeds the ordinating power of the far more consistent perspective from which they are viewed. Normalization necessarily tolerates the way we live now, but only to call vigilantly to mind the way we ought to. The current notion of a "dark" Trollope—insofar as it is anything more than a marketing ploy—only measures the depth of his assumption that, for basic purposes of socialization, a deontology is enough: the standards of a normalizing narration need not always or even often be incarnate in the narrative, since "deviant" data, too, pay tribute to the norm that saturates them with its values. Yet it is no less clear that any attempt to explicate these standards as so many injunctions (on the model of a legal code or an etiquette manual) must belie their textual status. Normalization in Trollope never issues from a single or constant source, but is rather floated across the text on a number of unlike supports, with none of which is it actually identified. It speaks variously in the voice of the novelist, of characters, of the fictive reader (not to mention the "dual voice" of *style indirect libre*), and in a mode that may be hyperbolic, direct, understated, or ironic. These multiple and overlapping instances contest, qualify, and reinforce one another—rather in the manner of moderate schism—to promote norms whose vagueness of origin and even of content helps make them ubiquitous. What emerges from the process are not commandments, but fields of problematization, in which behaviors are not so much judged as worried.

When Eleanor boxes Slope's ears, for example, it is an occasion for considerable fretting on the part of narrator and narratee alike. The well-bred reader, the writer fears, will now throw down the book in disgust. "She is a hoyden, one will say. At any rate she is not a lady, another will exclaim. I have suspected her all through, a third will declare; she has no idea of the dignity of a matron; or of the peculiar propriety which her position demands." The writer himself holds to a more scrupulous and nuanced view of the matter: Eleanor "cannot altogether be defended; and yet it may be averred that she is not a hoyden." And yet again, "It were to be wished devoutly that she had not struck Mr. Slope on the face. In doing so she derogated from her dignity and committed herself." Still, as far as Slope is concerned, "the slap on the face that he got from Eleanor was . . . the fittest rebuke which could have been administered to him." "But nevertheless, she should not have raised her hand against the man. Ladies' hands, so soft, so sweet, so delicious to the touch, so grateful to the eye, so gracious in their gentle doings, were not made to belabour men's faces" (389-90). All this, moreover, remains for real readers to fret about further. Both parties to the narrative contract (one will say) agree that a sin against propriety has been committed: the only question is whether the sin be mortal or venial, and it is easily answered, since Eleanor's own sense of guilt confirms the writer's defense of her against the well-bred reader's exaggerations. Yet (another will rejoin) Slope's rebuke is so clearly deserved that Trollope's treatment of the episode, including his remarks on ladies' hands, must be meant ironically to win our applause for Eleanor's spunk. What grounds, however, are there for speaking of irony (a third will demur) when Eleanor's "independence" is qualified here and elsewhere as "a feeling dangerous for a young woman" (390)? *E cosí via*—the game is afoot. On the one hand, the incident (ironic, or not, or ironic and not) is ordained to be the locus of a certain, albeit minor, controversy. On the other, even if its "moral" were agreed to be that "ladies' hands . . . were not made to belabour men's faces," this would be much less important than the prior consensus implied in the fuss that has put the incident under intensive moral consideration in the first place. That fuss, of course, situates Eleanor's gesture within a familiar code of propriety, on the Victorian-bourgeois horizon of class and gender expectations. Whatever we may think of her gesture, in order to think of it at all we cannot but keep in mind the code that inscribes it. And whatever we may think of this code— at least so long as we are readers of *Barchester Towers*—we can scarcely avoid thinking in it. Even when we subject it to various refinements and perversions, we remain caught in the closure of its own terms, which are thus perpetuated and revitalized. What Trollope describes in *Barchester Towers* is a world whose specific social problems are part of the general social solution that requires just such agitation to secure its consistency. What Trollope may be said to practice in *Barchester Towers* is a similarly socializing art of controversy, an art whose very interrogation of "problematic" behavior answers the need—where a police force is hardly feasible—for a common ground.

V

Since this common ground always doubles for a specific social organization, it is far from arbitrary which kinds or aspects of behavior are brought into question to support it. In this light, we might pursue the question of a woman's position—or rather the larger question of sexual difference that encompasses it. At its simplest (say, in the Grantly menage), sexual difference in *Barchester Towers* is posed as a variant of moderate schism, in which each uniquely determined sex makes love and war with the other, and both sexes cooperate accordingly to produce and reproduce the social. The asymmetries of power that the practice of moderate schism rehearses would here take the accumulated form of "patriarchy." Yet on the face of it, this basic structure is plagued with a major complication: the lines in the battle of the sexes are so frequently crossed (by virile females, by effeminate males) that Miss Thorne is not altogether implausible when she declares that "now-a-days the gentlemen were all women, and the ladies all men" (335). In fact, however, the phenomena she observes are regular effects of the structure that they scarcely render unintelligible. The Anglican Church, in contrast to either Roman Catholicism (whose priests are forbidden to marry) or early Methodism (where women were allowed to preach), provides Trollope with a lucid institutional model of patriarchy and its intrinsic discontents. Only men may occupy, solicit, and assign positions of power in this Church; at the same time, the men so entitled are all but made to share their lives with women, who are thus debarred from power even as they apparently need to be distributed throughout its organization. Part of women's patriarchal mission, this suggests, is to absorb a just dose of the homosocial affect required between men to maintain the institution: not so much of it, of course, that none is left over for its purpose, but neither so little of it that—as homosexuality, for instance—it unprofitably exceeds its function.[10] Patriarchal organization thus throws up two impediments to its own smooth functioning: the "strong" woman (who would be more than the socializing medium in the exchange and transfer of power between men) and the "weak" man (who, falling under the spell of such a woman, would imperil male bonding; or who, alternatively, fixated on male bonding per se, would endanger its social vocation).

In a liberal patriarchy, these figures must be tolerated; they would in any case be hard to eliminate from a social order that systematically produces them. But they are tolerated only insofar as they are immobilized as perennial "problem-types," sites of a critical concern so habitual that it can afford to be relaxed and amused. The gentleman-woman and the lady-man in Trollope are not symptoms of a patriarchy in disarray; nor do they imply a critique of the established gender code or an invitation to transsexual experimentation. Rather, they are the raw material for that massive stereotyping which, turning them into reminders of the gender norms they seem to transgress, makes radical transgression impossible. The virago, the siren, the "independent" woman (Mrs. Proudie, the Signora, Eleanor) are roles in the patriarchal image-repertory as stock as the ladies' man, the henpecked husband, the feckless father (Slope, Bishop Proudie, Harding). Trollope develops these roles with an easy confidence— as though it were not an emergency measure, but the routine task of liberal patriarchy to contain therein the dynamic that might otherwise issue in female "feminism" and male "homosexuality." In other words, if such terms are "anachronistic" applied to Trollope, it is because he is part of his culture's general effort to make them so. (*Encore un effort:* the terms remain utopian even in our day, when the groups they designate must still confront the difficulty of determining what their "own" discourse might be.)

It is easy to see, for example, that a standard of the "feminine" pervades the presentation of Mrs. Proudie, the Signora, and Eleanor, measuring whether, in what way, and to what degree they do or do not conform to it. The feminine, moreover, is not just an external norm, imposed on female characters like an oppression by a narration in which they necessarily have no say, or by other, male characters whose opinions may be supposed to be biased. It is also psychologically anchored in woman herself, at a point—all the more fitting if it is her "weak point"— where the "nature" she may try to avert returns to claim its rights and establish her truth. Thus, in her compassion for Mrs. Quiverful, Mrs. Proudie has "proved herself a woman" (241), and thereby for once wins our sympathy. The Signora, Trollope's chastened version of the self-sacrificing prostitute of continental literature, generously withdraws from competition "to give up Mr. Arabin to the woman whom he loved" (375)–as though she had perfectly absorbed from her reading of French novels the lesson of Balzac, Dumas, and Sue, that the only good "girl" is the one who knows she is bad. She condemns herself in the same bien-pensant terms her life only seems given over to mocking: "What would I not give to be loved by such a man [as Arabin]," she tells Eleanor, "that is, if I were an object fit for any man to love!" (446). And Eleanor herself–"the widow Bold"– comes to desire nothing better than to lose that appellation (which her baby-worship has never rendered very convincing): "She would give up the heavy burden of independence, and once more assume the position of a woman, and the duties of a trusting and loving wife" (478).

Yet perhaps these characters submit most deeply to patriarchy not when they acknowledge their latent femininity, but when they succeed in repressing it. For their only alternative to a femininity thoroughly circumscribed by its patriarchal determination seems to be a perverse identification with an oppressive masculinity equally and likewise circumscribed. Eleanor's decision to surrender her independence indicates, besides the extent to which she has been bought off, her understandable distaste for the world to which her independence has introduced her ("My name," she tells Arabin, "should never have been mixed up in your hostilities" [285]). Unlike her, of course, Mrs. Proudie embraces domination without scruple. Though the bishop may not be able to command her affections, they are altogether captivated by the male power game that she merely wants to play too. Her "petticoat government" only rather more successfully realizes the tyrannical fantasies of those who govern in trousers. Her ideal is as authoritarian as Slope's, and her character as machistic as Dr. Grantly's. In a different register, the Signora's siren act is also a willing assumption of the male power fantasies that have been literally pounded into her. Made by male violence to figure as the castrated woman ("maimed, lame, and . . . married" [253]), she returns the favor by playing to the hilt the role's other face: the castrating woman, with "dreadful eyes to look at" (69), and who, though lacking a leg, "is as full of mischief as tho' she had ten" (359). She positively cultivates the phallocentric metaphorics that determine her as the incomplete object of unfulfilled desire, as though she were cynically past caring that this rendered her the incomplete subject of unfulfilled desire as well. The "good-natured act" that "for once in her life" she resolves to perform (375) ought not to come as a surprise. Smitten once by a man's power, she is well prepared to be smitten a second time by a man's truth—by "the very spirit of truth" in which Arabin speaks to her (374). If the "feminist" is an impossible figure in *Barchester Towers,* it is because she has always already been seduced—by her own femininity, or—what comes to the same—by the male power and truth that determine it.

The trouble with a woman like Eleanor who boxes a man's ears is that, we recall, "she cannot altogether be defended." But if, having derogated from a proper feminine role, she cannot be defended, she must also have diminished a proper masculine role, which includes taking up her defense. The norm of femininity thus always presupposes a norm of masculinity, and the male characters in *Barchester Towers* are held to as stringent a gender ideal as the female. Slope's "broad chest and wide shoulders" (25), for instance, do not square the rap he takes for being (in the full ambiguity of the phrase) a ladies' man. Serenading "the softer sex" with "a soft word" and "that low silky whisper which he had always specially prepared for feminine ears" (24, 56), he becomes so soft himself that when "the priestly charmer" (28) meets his match in another "Italianised charmer" (122), he cannot manfully defend against her wiles, but yields to passion in the best feminine style. The implied accusation of effeminacy is not far removed from the charge of "latent homosexuality" that it will become a tradition to lay at

the door of the Don Juan. And what better partner with whom
to arraign Slope on these grounds than the emasculated bishop,
"the little man" (125) so diminutive that Dr. Grantly, if he
liked, might pat him on the head (486)?

> [The bishop's] little idea of using Mr. Slope as a counterpoise to his
> wife had well nigh evaporated. He had all but acknowledged the futility
> of the scheme. If indeed he could have slept in his chaplain's bed-room
> instead of his wife's, there might have been something in it. But——.
> (304)

If the "feminist" needs to be seduced, the "homosexual" needs
to be abandoned—to the derision of Trollope's joke, and worse,
to the impossibility of its "But——." The comfortable, clubby
wit is just what is required, since it is the comfort of the club
that might otherwise have been at stake. The euphoric moment
in the normative experience of homosocial patriarchy comes not
simply when "the ivy has found its tower" (477), and Eleanor
accepted Arabin, but after Arabin has communicated the news
to another man. " 'It's just as I would have it,' " says Grantly,
holding Arabin "fast by the hand."

> And as he finished speaking, a tear might have been observed in each of
> the doctor's eyes.
>   Mr. Arabin warmly returned the archdeacon's grasp, but he said little.
> His heart was too full for speaking, and he could not express the grati-
> tude which he felt. Dr. Grantly understood him as well as though he
> had spoken for an hour.
>   "And mind, Arabin," said he, "no one but myself shall tie the knot."
> (487)

The "fast" hand-holding, the unfallen tears, the tacit expression
of gratitude—all such details indulge the affect of male bonding
even as they overcome the femininity with which it must never
be confused—or at least not until the bonding subjects, like the
odd, loving couple formed by Harding and Bishop Grantly, are
old enough to have already performed their social functions.

VI

When I read Trollope, it is all I can do not to be bored. All I can do, because Trollope always seems a little bored himself. What produces this impression is his habitual manner of rendering the stuff of his fiction matter of course, of dressing it in an ever-familiar uniform. "A morning party is a bore" (401). We may not have known this before, but if we know it now, we know it too well: in the mode, not of an insight owing to the novelist's penetration, but of a truism that he merely passes along. From the boredom of a world whose phenomena are universally sedated in the routinized perception of them "as usual" derives the comfort that Trollope is known to administer. But boredom, as the example of pornography perhaps best illustrates, overtakes not what is intrinsically dull, but what is "interesting" to excess. Far from the simple reflex-response to banality, boredom hysterically converts into yawning affectlessness what would otherwise be outright panic. When I read Trollope—when, in other words, the individual subject reads the generality that abolishes him—it is all I can do to refuse my impending boredom: to convert it back into the anxiety that it is meant to bind, to insist on the shock that it is the attempt to meet and parry. And should one recognize Trollope for the proper name of a cultural strategy that is still "boring" us, boring through us (though the Novel is no longer the primary site or instrument of the drill), the shock would only widen.[11]

NOTES

1. Anthony Trollope, *Barchester Towers*, The World's Classics (London: Oxford University Press, 1960), pp. 25 and 148. All subsequent references to this novel are to this edition and are cited parenthetically in the text by page number.

2. See "A Study on Authority," in Herbert Marcuse, *From Luther to Popper* (London: New Left Books, 1972), pp. 49-155.

3. The process is perhaps best represented in Dickens's *David Copperfield,* where David's early experiences at Salem House and at Murdstone and Grinby's are sublated in the formation of his later self-discipline. See D. A. Miller, "Secret Subjects, Open Secrets," *Dickens Studies Annual* 14 (1985): 17-38.

4. Michel Foucault, "Two Lectures," in *Power/Knowledge,* ed. Colin Gordon (New York: Pantheon Books, 1981), p. 90. Two other texts by Foucault also deserve mention for their bearing on my later discussion of the novelistic pastorate: "Omnes et Singulatim: Towards a Criticism of 'Political Reason,'" in *The Tanner Lectures on Human Value,* ed. S. M. McMurrin, 2 vols. (Cambridge: Cambridge University Press, 1980-81), 2:223-54; and "The Subject and Power," *Critical Inquiry* 8 (Summer 1982): 777-95.

5. Franco Moretti, *Signs Taken for Wonders* (London: New Left Books, 1983), p. 243n.

6. Anthony Trollope, *An Autobiography,* The World's Classics (London: Oxford University Press, 1953), pp. 199-200.

7. Anthony Trollope, *The Warden,* The World's Classics (London: Oxford University Press, 1961), p. 186.

8. Trollope, *Autobiography,* p. 200.

9. Ibid.

10. Eve Kosofsky Sedgwick, to whom I owe much in what follows, would frankly call this homosocial affect *desire,* and thus insist on "the potential unbrokenness of a continuum between homosocial and homosexual—a continuum whose visibility, for men, in our society, is radically disrupted" (*Between Men: English Literature and Male Homosocial Desire* [New York: Columbia University Press, 1985], pp. 1-2).

11. Paul de Man would have been the last to claim that puns are personal property, but that what painfully wearies may also no less painfully pierce was suggested to me by a remark he once made on Baudelairean *ennui.* I am less casually indebted to the suggestions of Marston Anderson, Ann Bermingham, Mitchell Breitwieser, Carol T. Christ, Neil Hertz, Caroline Newman, and Alex Zwerdling, who kindly read this essay in various drafts.

Catherine Gallagher

George Eliot and *Daniel Deronda:*
The Prostitute and the Jewish Question

I would like to reopen a question that seems to have been prematurely closed: What conception of authorship, what ideas about its nature, simultaneously attracted hundreds of English women to that career in the nineteenth century and severely handicapped them in practicing it? Many of you will immediately think that this question, of all questions about women writers, has been amply answered, for you will recall that Sandra Gilbert and Susan Gubar, as well as numerous other feminist critics, point to the historical association of authorship with generative paternity.[1] Women, presumably, were driven to write in order to "create" for themselves, but they found that the male metaphor of literary creativity—the patriarchal metaphor—excluded them from the province of letters, and their books consequently rehearse this sense of exclusion and handicapped (castrated) creativity. Such an analysis concentrates on the historical connections linking author, father, and male God to the exclusion of all other associations that might have occurred to nineteenth-century writers.

Moreover, the critics themselves seem to subscribe to the underlying association of writing with creative generativity. They are merely offended that women were thought unfit for this procreative art. Although these critics sometimes suggest that the male myth of the generative Word was designed to compensate for the fictional nature of all fatherhood, they seldom carry this critique of creativity very far, and remain content to point out that generativity is a "naturally" female characteristic, implying that the natural metaphor of the mother-author was the very thing the patriarchal metaphor was designed to preempt.

I would like to argue that another, very different association also helped structure the conjunction of gender and authorship in the nineteenth century. When women entered the career of authorship, they did not enter an inappropriately male territory, but a degradingly female one. They did not need to find a female metaphor for authorship; they needed to avoid or transform the one that was already there. The historical association—disabling, empowering and central to nineteenth-century consciousness— that I would like to discuss is not the metaphor of the writer as father, but the metaphor of the author as whore.

This metaphor has an ancient pedigree. Classicists tell us that although few women in the Greek classical period actually wrote, the association of writing with femaleness in general and prostitution in particular spread with the increase in literacy itself. A link between writing and malevolent forms of female power can be found in several fragments; a too-close association with letters was also believed to emasculate a man.[2] Underlying these associations is a notion of written language far removed from the idea of the procreative Word. It has been noted that Aristotle was uncertain about whether writing most resembled the natural generativity of plants and animals or the unnatural generation of money, which, in usury, proliferates through mere circulation but brings nothing qualitatively new into being. At times, Aristotle speaks of poetic making as a method of natural reproduction; at other times, he speaks of the written word as an arbitrary and conventional sign multiplying unnaturally in the mere process of exchange. The former idea of language promotes the metaphor of literary paternity; the latter the metaphor of literary usury[3] and, ultimately, literary prostitution.

The whole sphere to which usury belongs, the sphere of exchange as opposed to that of production, is traditionally associated with women. Women are items of exchange, a form of currency and also a type of commodity. Of course, in normal kinship arrangements, when the exchange is completed and the woman becomes a wife, she enters the realm of "natural" (in the Aristotelian sense) production. But the prostitute never makes this transition from exchange to production; she retains her commodity form at all times. Like money, the prostitute, according to ancient accounts, is incapable of natural procreation. For all her sexual activity, indeed because of all of her sexual activity, she fails to bring new substances, children, into the world.[4] Her womb, it seems, is too slippery. And yet she is a source of proliferation. What multiplies through her, though, is not a substance but a sign: money. Prostitution, then, like usury, is a metaphor for one of the ancient models of linguistic production: the unnatural multiplication of interchangeable signs.

From ancient times, then, we have evidence of two radically different ways of thinking about authors, one based on a masculine metaphor, the other on a feminine metaphor. Both are associated with forms of multiplication, of proliferation, and yet they cannot be made parallel, for they operate on completely different assumptions about the nature of linguistic procreation. The gender distinction in literary theory is not between male fathers who *can* multiply and female eunuchs who *cannot,* not between male language and female silence, but between the natural production of new things in the world and the "unnatural" reproduction of mere signs. According to the father metaphor, the author generates real things in the world through language; according to the whore metaphor, language proliferates itself in a process of exchange through the author.

This essay does not attempt to choose between these metaphors or to develop an abstract truth about authorship. Rather, it describes specific historical associations confronting professional women writers in the nineteenth century, when the metaphor of the author as whore was commonplace. My purpose, then, is to register the peculiar Victorian resonances of the metaphor and to use it as a way both of interpreting the ending of George Eliot's career and of understanding her last novel, *Daniel Deronda.*

As in classical times, prostitution in the nineteenth century is linked to writing through their joint inhabitation of the realm of exchange. It is impossible to specify one universally accepted

Victorian idea of the way exchange functions inside the general economy, but we can venture to assert that the processes of exchange, of circulation, are distinguished from those of production by all political economists. The sphere of production, rather than that of circulation, is then identified as the source of value, the source of real wealth. The Marxist critique of political economy, with its distinction between the production and realization of surplus-value, only refines the qualitative difference between these economic realms. These realms, of course, interpenetrate, for the essence of capitalism, as both political economists and their critics agree, is production that depends on the exchange of two underlying commodities: labor (or labor-power) and money. The stated source of value (and of surplus-value), however, remains the productive labor of the worker, that which brings some new things into the world.

Nineteenth-century economic thought, then, systematically accords the processes of exchange an epiphenomenal status even as it conceives of exchange as the ever-present condition of production. The marketplace (as distinct from the workplace) is truly a mechanism of *realization:* value is a shadowy potential until it is realized in exchange, but exchange only realizes the value already created in production. Circulation can never be a source of value. If in usury money seems to multiply through exchange alone, we are told, that is mere illusion, for all increases in wealth depend on someone's labor.

Those who hold this labor theory of value must wish the marketplace to be a simple reflection of values established in the productive sphere. The free market desired by laissez-faire political economists is first and foremost a market in labor, and the price of labor should determine, in the final analysis, the price of other commodities. A market unresponsive to that determination or overly responsive to other determinations is what much nineteenth-century economic theory is designed to do away with. A marketplace not directly bound to production, the value of a commodity wildly incommensurate with the value of the labor embodied in the commodity, is almost universally regarded as a bad thing. And as this economic discourse finds more popular expressions in either the liberal or the socialist traditions, one detects a growing hostility toward groups that seem to represent a realm of exchange divorced from production: for example, traders in general but especially costermongers in works like Mayhew's *London Labour and the London Poor,* prostitutes in the works of Mayhew, Acton, W. R. Greg and others, and Jews in the works of almost everybody.

The latter two representatives, the prostitute and the almost always Jewish usurer, are ubiquitous in nineteenth-century writing about authorship. Examples abound, from Sainte-Beuve's often-quoted remark that all persons of renown are prostitutes, to Thackeray's ironic defense of Eugène Sue: "He gets half-a-crown a line for this bad stuff, and has, one may say with certainty, a hundred thousand readers every day. Many a man and author has sold himself for far less."[5] The activities of authoring, of procuring illegitimate income, and of alienating one's self through prostitution seem particularly closely associated with one another in the Victorian period. Thackeray identifies two reasons for this historical conjuncture: the development of cheap serial publication (in which authors were often paid by the line) and the growth of a massive popular readership in the 1830s and 1840s. These conditions most directly affected what we now call popular literature, but the decreasing cost of publication, advances in education, and changes in copyright law made it impossible for any professional writer to claim to be independent of the marketplace. The author, moreover, does not go to market as a respectable producer with an alienable commodity, but with *himself or herself* as commodity. The last half of the eighteenth century is the period both when the identity of text and self begins to be strongly asserted and when the legal basis for commodifying texts (as distinct from books) comes into being in copyright law. This combination puts writers in the marketplace in the position of selling themselves, like whores.

If, on the other hand, writers refrain from identifying their true selves with their texts, they get caught in another strand of the web of exchange, for language itself, especially published writing, is then often identified with money as an alien, artificial, and entrapping system of circulation. In Thackeray's *Pendennis* and Trollope's *The Way We Live Now,* for example, literary exchange resembles usury and inflationary retailing. It should be noted, moreover, that the Victorian usurious writer is often female and thus a composite image of usurer and whore. Many nineteenth-century statements about the false, imitative, and merely conventional nature of women's writing, statements that have been used to prove that the woman writer was considered a eunuch, should be reread with these metaphors of exchange in mind. For each indignant outburst against female authors emphasizes these authors' unearned ascendancy in the marketplace. George Eliot's "Silly Novels by Lady Novelists," W. R. Greg's falsely moral women novelists, and Hawthorne's scribbling women are all distinguished from productive laborers. Eliot is most emphatic about this distinction in her essay (1856) in which she argues that "'In all labour there is profit;' but ladies' silly novels, we imagine, are less the result of labour than of busy idleness."[6]

These women do not, then, inhabit the sphere of literary *production,* but that is only half of their sin. The other half lies in the fact that they are nevertheless prolific. Their novels sell, and what is more, they sell because they merely recirculate a conventional language. The ladies, Eliot tells us, "are remarkably unanimous in their choice of diction";[7] their characters and incidents, she claims, are also identical. All the matter, she emphasizes, is drawn from novels and goes back into the making of more novels. Such women rake off profits without production, without labor.

The links George Eliot made between a certain kind of female literature, inflation, dishonest retailing, and usurious exchange were common, and easily called to mind the woman of pure exchange, the woman as commodity, the prostitute. What is surprising about Eliot, however, is her claim that exchange is the essence of all authorship. Eliot's dominant metaphor for authorship, both in her novels and essays, is not genealogy but commerce. And her commercial language often stresses exchange over production. For example, in her note on "Authorship," written sometime in the 1870s, she not only describes authorship in metaphors of exchange but also defines it as an act of commodity circulation. In this note, she plays down the role of production by baldly stating that writing is not the author's definitive activity. To be an author, she explains, is a social activity, a "bread winning profession," whereas merely "to write prose or verse as a private exercise and satisfaction is not a social activity."[8] "Social" here means, first of all, economic. In this note, as in numerous other notes and essays throughout her career, Eliot identifies the characteristics of her chosen profession, and the first characteristic is its location in the marketplace. The difference between the mere writer and the author is that the author writes for money.

Since mere writing is not a social act, the note on "Authorship" tells us, "nobody is culpable" for it. Writing is innocent; publication is guilty and also perilous. As Eliot presents them in numerous late essays, authors are the creatures of an economy that constantly imperils their identities and their products. In other markets, she claims, production and exchange are harmoniously coordinated; in the literary market, however, they are at odds. That which defines the authors, exchange, always also seeks to undo them, to make them profitable but unproductive. The market will encourage the author to recirculate, "to do over again what has already been done, either by himself or others."[9] This danger is elaborated by Eliot through the usury metaphor in her *Theophrastus Such* essays.[10]

The *Theophrastus Such* essays also construct the threat of the prostituting, "amusing" author who purveys poison, spreads disease, and generates unnatural passions and excessive appetites.

In "Debasing the Moral Currency," for example, burlesques of great literature are first likened to an inflated currency and then to an inflamed woman with a combustible liquid: "I confess," writes the essayist, "that sometimes when I see a certain style of young lady, who checks our tender admiration with rouge and henna and all the blazonry of an extravagant expenditure, with slang and bold *brusquerie* intended to signify her emancipated view of things, and with cynical mockery which she mistakes for penetration, I am sorely tempted to hiss out *'Petroleuse'!*" [11] Here the image of *Liberté* as a whore emerges directly out of the liberty of the cultural marketplace.

The inflationary usurer and the infectious or combustible "expensive" woman—these are the assured but dangerous inhabitants of the authorial sphere, the degradingly feminine sphere of exchange. Why did Eliot so insistently place authors in this unsavory company by emphasizing their dependence on circulation? What deep attraction drew Eliot to the commercial definition despite its perils? The answer is twofold. The first and most obvious reply takes us back to a consideration of why, initially, loose women are associated with the marketplace. Money may be a sign of sterility and even of an outcast status, but it is nevertheless an emblem of liberation from patriarchal authority. The woman in the marketplace is presumably free from the patriarch, both in the sense that she needs the permission and approval of no single man and in the sense that finding her determination in the nexus of relationships with clients or the public enables her to escape the identity imposed by a father. By associating herself with the marketplace, Eliot evades any specifically patriarchal authority that her literal and her literary forefathers might try to impose, replacing the mystifications of genealogy with the realities of economics.

The commercial definition of authorship, though, has an even more complex role in Eliot's discourse. Established as a *fact,* it creates the necessity for its own transcendence in the realm of *value.* By defining the author as a writer in the marketplace,

Eliot not only minimizes the anxiety attached to one metaphor but also establishes a different metaphoric core of anxiety for her own work. The guilt of illegitimate genealogical appropriation may be occluded, but the guilt of usurious and whorish commercial appropriation then immediately opens up.

This, however, is a profitable opening for Eliot. For out of it emerges the demand for a different economy, a demand constantly stimulated but never quite met by her own texts. By relentlessly exposing the unnaturalness of the commercial literary economy—its severance from "real wants" and independence of standards of quality in the commodity—Eliot promotes the artificial construction of a superseding *moral* economy.

But although the perils of the commercial economy that necessitate the moral economy are elaborately detailed in the late essays and poems, the moral economy itself remains vague. From the note on "Authorship," we learn that the moral economy would ensure "real" productivity, for it would regulate publication on the basis of quality. Good work, moreover, would add a truly new substance to the world, would make "a real contribution."[12] And yet, despite these appeals to originality, Eliot never equates productivity with natural generation. One of the few things the late essays make clear about the moral economy of culture is its sharp separation from nature. The most dangerous belief afoot, Theophrastus Such tells us, is that identified by Sainte-Beuve, the belief "that culture is something innate, that it is the same thing as nature."[13]

The moral economy, then, must break with the commercial literary economy and yet remain an economy, a sphere of exchange. Eliot's last novel, *Daniel Deronda,* allows us to investigate the problematic implications of this double imperative and to see why, within the terms of Eliot's discourse, cosmopolitan culture finally fails to be that sufficiently differentiated sphere.

Daniel Deronda displays the same preoccupations as Eliot's other late works. Usury, prostitution, and art become, in the course of the novel, interchangeable activities. They are made not identical, but fungible with each other by a complex pattern of metaphors, plot reversals, and ironic exchanges too intricate to describe here. Perhaps the most instructive part of this pattern, though, is the figure that Daniel himself makes in it. Daniel, the supposed saint and savior, is the novel's major negotiator of these exchanges and the only character who stands for each activity of exchange in turn.

Daniel Deronda opens on a cosmopolitan world of pure exchange and immediately introduces the major representatives of that sphere: the beautiful but sinister and reckless woman and the Jewish pawnbroker. The gambling casino at Leubrunn, which functions, the epigraph tells us, as the medium rather than the origin of the story, is a society itself mediated by a roulette wheel. When that wheel is in motion, it suspends normal social distinctions and creates an ironic momentary Utopia of equality at the expense of fraternity. The roulette game is a mystified, abstracted, and grotesquely passive war of all against all. The various players, as seen through Daniel's eyes, see only the roulette wheel and do not see one another. The wheel seems to make money appear and disappear, but in reality, the players are only exchanging money, as Daniel later explains to Gwendolen; one's gain is another's loss in this form of nonproductive money-getting. Like all money gained in the realm of pure exchange, roulette winnings are a double sign of credit and debit.

They are, indeed, exactly like the profits the Jewish pawnbroker makes from the exchange of Gwendolen Harleth's necklace in the very next episode; and it is this identity that underlies the irony of Gwendolen's bitter reflection that "these Jew dealers were so unscrupulous in taking advantage of Christians unfortunate at play!"[14] The business of the Jew and the play of the Christian are altogether isomorphic, and their symmetry derives from the doubleness of the sought-after sign: the nine louis given to Gwendolen in exchange for her necklace, like all signs in usurious exchange, represent a double indebtedness. From Gwendolen's point of view, the nine louis represent a loss;

she feels she has not been paid enough for the necklace. In her mind, the Jew really owes her something—has something of hers that is worth more than she has been paid; from the usurer's point of view, Gwendolen has merely prepaid a debt to him that she would have incurred for the use of his money.

This vast game of beggar-your-neighbor, in which the debtors can claim to be the creditors, and vice versa, is Gwendolen's natural sphere. At least, as we first see her through Daniel's eyes, she seems particularly appropriate to it because she is herself a double sign. The book opens with the questions: "Was she beautiful or not beautiful? . . . Was the good or the evil genius dominant?" (35). Daniel concludes, "Probably the evil," and then goes on to "save" Gwendolen by increasing the minus side of her account.

In this way, Daniel, through his very disapproval, enters into an exchange with Gwendolen that pairs him with the pawn-broker. Gwendolen herself makes the association when she remembers that Daniel's hotel is in the same street as the pawn-broker's shop; she imagines Daniel scrutinizing and evaluating her as Mr. Wiener scrutinizes and evaluates her jewels. But surely, it might be objected, this pairing of Daniel with the pawnbroker is a pairing of opposites, as Daniel's immediate retrieval and restoration of the necklace make clear. Daniel sends Gwendolen two items along with the redeemed necklace: (1) a supposedly anonymous note saying, "A stranger who has found Miss Har-leth's necklace returns it to her with the hope that she will not again risk the loss of it," and (2) a handkerchief from which "a large corner . . . seemed to have been recklessly torn off to get rid of a mark" (49). The whole packet comprises a message that seems to say the opposite of what a pawn ticket, a promissory note, or, indeed, any kind of money generally says. For the signs Daniel sends Gwendolen represent not the promise to pay of a specified person or government, but an acknowledgment that an ostentatiously anonymous person (a stranger, a recklessly torn off mark, the sign of a flamboyantly discarded identity) has already paid. They resemble, then, an anonymous receipt closing a particular transaction, but their prohibition against exchange also extends beyond the immediate transaction, making them a species of anti-money. They are a specific directive against further exchange: the stranger hopes that Miss Harleth "will not again risk the loss" of the necklace by pawning it. Moreover, since the necklace is made of stones that had belonged to Gwendolen's father, their return, accompanied by Daniel's stern note, could easily be seen as the valorization of genealogy over exchange: the father orders the daughter to vacate the marketplace and remain dependent on his legacy alone.

Superficially, then, Daniel and the pawnbroker are a pair of opposites. And yet if we consider the effect of Daniel's actions on Gwendolen, his exchanges with her only make him a more formidable version of the usurer. Gwendolen quite rightly refuses to see his package as a restoration of her loss; it represents, rather, the further depletion of her self-esteem. She can no longer fancy that the pawnbroker owes her something. By buying back the necklace, at the usurer's higher price, and then returning it to her, Daniel increases her deficit by putting her in debt to him. The signs that he sends Gwendolen—the necklace, the note, and the handkerchief—replace the usurious signs of double indebtedness with tokens of unidirectional, unambiguous debt. In attempting to get rid of her doubleness, Daniel vastly increases Gwendolen's indebtedness and makes it impossible for her to repay him. Since the note is anonymous, she cannot even object to the liberty Daniel has taken without exposing herself to humiliation. Finally, she can only quit the scene of these encounters with a sense of permanent and demeaning disadvantage. If Daniel redeems anyone in this exchange, he redeems the pawnbroker, whose profits are realized and whose debts are canceled. And that is in summary the plot of the whole novel: a young man who thinks he has a mission to save wayward women turns out to have a mission to save a nation of usurers.

Daniel's warning to Gwendolen, furthermore, only drives her

from one arena of exchange to another. Unlike Leubrunn, which gives Gwendolen fantasies of escaping the determinations of her sex, the English marketplace to which she returns is explicitly sexual and contaminated by illicit relationships. Henleigh Grandcourt seeks Gwendolen as a *wife* and not a mistress, but the novel purposely collapses this distinction, reverses the terms by a series of exchanges, and proves that a wife can be a prostitute both in her own eyes and in those of her husband. By knowingly taking the place of, allowing herself to be exchanged for, Grandcourt's mistress, Lydia Glasher, Gwendolen becomes a sign of the very thing she is not, the abandoned woman of passion, the mistress, the whore. It is this identification through exchange that repels Gwendolen, and it is this identification to which she must ultimately submit. By being exchanged with the woman of exchange in her marriage to Grandcourt, she will remain forever a sign of exchange and, in her own mind at least, a sign of the very illicit sexuality she cannot herself enjoy.

Gwendolen is finally transformed into a commodity condemned to perpetual resale to the same consumer, a state maintained by the periodic checks Grandcourt sends her mother. Her new status is traumatically forced on her consciousness by the receipt, on her wedding night, of yet another package, this one from Lydia Glasher. Like Daniel's earlier package, it also contains jewels and a note. In a sense, Lydia's package cancels Daniel's because this time the note emphasizes that the enclosed jewels are not legitimately Gwendolen's. The note reads, "These diamonds, which were once given with ardent love to Lydia Glasher, she passes on to you. You have broken your word to her, that you might possess what was hers . . . The man you have married has a withered heart. His best young love was mine; you could not take that from me when you took the rest. It is dead; but I am the grave in which your chance of happiness is buried as well as mine" (406). The box, now a casket full of diamonds, continues to stand for Lydia Glasher's passionate sexuality, which has been taken from her but cannot therefore be bestowed on Gwendolen. The note insists that Gwendolen receive the box as simply one payment for the alienation of her own sexuality, an alienation that must be perpetually transacted with the same man. In thus paying Gwendolen, Lydia also pays her back, with a vengeance, emphasizing that Gwendolen's very lack of passion, her lack of any but a financial motive for marrying Grandcourt, makes her the real whore and simultaneously denies her the whore's pleasure and freedom.

Unlike Daniel's package, then, Lydia's package tells Gwendolen that there is no way out. She does not have a choice between fatherly authority and alienating exchanges. The father is dead and yet lives on in the very exchanges that seemed before to mark his liberating absence. But if, once again, we look at the way these two packages function in Gwendolen's psychic development, we can see that they are very similar. Lydia's act resembles Daniel's because it, too, establishes a unidirectional, unambiguous debt that can never be repaid. If Daniel's first pairing in the narrative is with the pawnbroker, his second is with Lydia Glasher, the illicitly sexual woman. And this identification sharpens as the novel progresses, for Gwendolen (like almost everyone else in the book) thinks Daniel is the illegitimate son of Sir Hugo Mallinger, whose legal heir (because Sir Hugo has failed to produce a legitimate son) is Henleigh Grandcourt. Gwendolen thus identifies Grandcourt's displacement of Daniel with her own displacement of Lydia and Lydia's children. Both Daniel and Gwendolen think of Daniel as the representative of the illicitly sexual and wronged woman.

Through two kinds of illicit sexual exchange, then, the characters in *Daniel Deronda* themselves become interchangeable, not because they are reduced to uniformity but because, like money, they expand into doubleness. They come to mean what they are not; loss and gain are reversed. Daniel and Gwendolen especially become legible to each other only by an understanding of their mutual illegitimacy. And "illegitimacy" is the word neither can say because it conjures up the secret signified of both, that which is embodied, or rather disembodied, in the elusive creature, Daniel's missing mother. She is the central mystery in the novel, the woman with an "enigmatic veiled face," who fills not just Daniel's imagination, but Gwendolen's too, with "dread" and "shame" (206). They think, and we think, that their own lives refer to hers and that hers refers to dreadful, shameful sexuality. They think, and we think, that this sexuality causes the problems of identity and alienation from which they both suffer, deprives them of a stable ground, and makes them both, in different ways, reluctant signs of things antithetical to them.

It seems an odd twist, then, when the dreadful, shameful veiled core of meaning to which so much in the novel alludes turns out not to be a loose woman, a public or private concubine, but an *artist,* the greatest lyric actress of her time. All through his life, Daniel has thought that he stood as the sign of his mother's sexual sin; in the climax of the novel, however, he finds that his life means something else entirely. Instead of having been abandoned as a sign of shameful sex, Daniel was literally traded for an artistic career; he is, in this sense, the representative of his mother's career because he is the thing that she exchanged for it. Daniel is just like the little boy we briefly glimpse in the opening chapter, who stands with his back to the gaming table as his mother plays: "He alone had his face turned towards the doorway, and fixing on it the blank gaze of a bedizened child stationed as a masquerading advertisement on the platform of an itinerant show, stood close behind a lady deeply engaged at the roulette-table" (36). Daniel and the little boy stand for the play by having been left for it. As the reader's mind later takes in the fact that the metaphorical roulette-table means artistic rather than sexual exchange, the interchangeability of these two activities is reasserted.

"Reasserted," rather than asserted, because, long before Daniel's mother is unveiled, the novel repeatedly emphasizes the close connection between selling oneself as a sexual commodity and selling oneself as an artist. The points of connection in the narrative are too numerous to list completely, but the most obvious and often-remarked instances are the degenerate actor Lapidoth's attempt to pander his daughter Mirah, first as a singer and then as a prostitute, and Gwendolen's proposal to go on the stage just before she sells herself to Grandcourt. The constant association of Gwendolen's affinity for the stage and her desire to remain in the realm of exchange strengthen the same connection on a somewhat more abstract level.

But although these connections are obvious, their implications are not. What is the nature and extent of the identification between prostitution and art in *Daniel Deronda?* With the entrance of the Alcharisi, the novel seems intent on making a universal association between artists and prostitutes, one component of which is the very difference between them. The Alcharisi was as dedicated to artistic traditions as Herr Klesmer, the novel's explicit example of a pure and authentic artist. Hers was the long and arduous apprenticeship that Gwendolen is incapable of. Hers too was the natural power lacking in Mirah. Her training and genius, it would seem, save her from the threat of prostitution that both Gwendolen and Mirah face. Indeed, all three women's stories indicate that art and prostitution are *alternatives* in women's lives, but alternatives with such similar structures that their very alternativeness calls attention to their interchangeability.

The structural similarity between the two careers emphasized in the Alcharisi's story is their joint exclusion of generational reproduction. Like a prostitute, the Alcharisi is a slippery womb out of which Daniel has fallen. Thus Daniel does, in a sense, represent her preference for many men over one: "Men followed me from one country to another. I was living a myriad lives in one. I did not want a child" (688–89). Similarly, she emphasizes that her entry into a cultural marketplace freed her from becoming a mere link in a family line: "[My father] wished I had been a son; he cared for me as a makeshift link. . . . He hated that Jewish women should be thought of by the Christian world as a sort of ware to make public singers and actresses of. As if we were not the more enviable for that! That is a chance of escaping from bondage" (694).

Both the woman artist and the prostitute, then, are established in the sphere of exchange that excludes "natural" generation and substitutes for it an exhilaratingly dangerous love affair with a multitude. The female performer, as a contemporary noted, must "sacrifice maiden modesty or matronly reserve" in order to be "stared at, commented on, clapped or hissed by a crowded and often unmannered audience, who forget the woman in the artist."[15] This immediate and threatening relationship to the cultural consumer, though, is only one of the ways in which the performer acts out the relationship between art and exchange. Another aspect of performance recalls the metaphor of the usurer and further breaks down the distinction not only between kinds of artist but also between the repulsive and admirable elements of their art. It is, indeed, a single trait of the performer that makes her both type and antitype of the artist. The performer, according to an 1875 essay by George Henry Lewes, which seems to state both his and Eliot's opinion on the topic, is a mere medium for other artists. He is only a painted thing, Lewes complains, who simply *represents* the creation of the poet.[16] The word *represent,* emphasized in Lewes's essay, is used repeatedly about Alcharisi: "All feeling," we are told, "immediately became matter of conscious representation" for her; "I cared for the wide world," she tells her son, "and what I could represent in it" (691). Never is she described as an originator of substance. Lewes's essay goes on to argue that actors command too high a price, both in fame and money. Their market values, he insists, are inflated, for they are only "luxuries."[17] The performer, then, is another instance of the usurious artist who dominates Eliot's late work. It is thus little wonder that Jews have only two professions in this book. The Alcharisi reports that her husband, Daniel's father, "wound up his money changing . . . and lived to wait upon me" (696).

But it is this same element of theatrical performance that makes Eliot use it as a synecdoche for what is best in art. The performance requires the submergence of the self in the words and thoughts of another; it requires, then, the development of the kind of self Eliot considered ideal, the "self that self restrains" in the interests of some larger, corporate identity. To forget the woman in the artist, to become the medium of the collective project of culture, Eliot often argues, is to enable the spiritual economy. Every time she invokes the usury metaphor, then, or refers to the inauthentic and parasitic nature of theatrical performance, she raises objections to that very moral economy of art she elsewhere invokes.

In *Daniel Deronda* we can see Eliot struggling with this contradiction and only resolving it finally by separating the moral economy from art. For the novel shows us that artistic exchange, even when separated from monetary exchange, produces effects very like those of financial circulation. In "The Modern Hep! Hep! Hep!," the last of the *Theophrastus Such* essays, Eliot sums up those effects in the word "alienism." Alienism is a spiritual disease that, she tells us, is sometimes euphemistically called "cosmopolitanism." Jews are particularly prone to it because, having no homeland of their own, they are often forced to live in the medium of abstract universalism created by international finance. Although Eliot argues that the Jews have not yet been made "viciously cosmopolitan by holding the world's money-bag," and hence resolving "all national interests" into "the algebra of loans," she fears that such cosmopolitanism would result from any relaxation of their separatism.[18] If Jews are to be virtuous, she insists, they must have at least a spiritual nationality and at best a reconstituted homeland.

Money, however, is not the only breeder of "alienism," a word with striking Arnoldian resonances. In *Culture and Anarchy*, Arnold called his bearers of culture, his "saving remnant," "aliens," and called upon the English to overcome their insularity and embrace the "best that has been thought and said" no matter

what its origin.[19] In "The Modern Hep! Hep! Hep!" it is precisely this sort of cultural internationalism that Eliot deplores:
"A common humanity is not yet enough to feed the rich blood
of various activity which makes a complete man. The time is
not come for cosmopolitanism to be highly virtuous . . . It is
admirable in a Briton with a good purpose to learn Chinese, but
it would not be a proof of fine intellect in him to taste Chinese
poetry in the original more than he tastes the poetry of his own
tongue."[20]

The character who suffers from this aspect of culture in *Daniel Deronda* is Daniel himself—Daniel, whose first inklings of
identity came through books and who is disempowered by a *too*
diffuse sympathy, a lack of particularity always associated with
the decentering power of wide reading: "His imagination had so
wrought itself to the habit of seeing things as they probably appeared to others, that a strong partisanship, unless it were against
an immediate oppression, had become an insincerity for him . . .
A too reflective and diffusive sympathy was in danger of paralys-
ing in him that indignation against wrong and that selectedness
of fellowship which are the conditions of moral force." He seeks
an "influence that would justify partiality" (412–13). Ironically,
in depriving him of his Jewishness, his mother has turned him
into another version of the Jew: the cultured cosmopolitan, the
alien.

By embracing Jewish nationalism, then, Daniel saves the Jews
and himself from abstract universalism. He will save them, it is
hoped, from money, and himself from cosmopolitan culture, by
replacing both with the mystic merger of souls described in the
Cabbala. Eliot is drawn to the Cabbala for its principle of exchange, but she never confuses this with the exchanges of authorship. "In the doctrine of the Cabbala," Mordecai explains to
Daniel, "souls are born again and again in new bodies till they
are perfected and purified, and a soul liberated from a worn-out
body may join the fellow-soul that needs it. . . . When my long-
wandering soul is liberated from this weary body, it will join

yours, and its work will be perfected" (599–600). This is the moral economy for which both money-changing and art are exchanged in *Daniel Deronda.* The substitution is effected, once again, through an exchange of jewelry; Daniel's ring, which had been his money-changing father's, had been given to him by his artistic mother, and had provided him entrée into the pawnshop of Ezra Cohen, is taken by the pander Lapidoth as a kind of payment for his children. This alienation of all the negative things Jewishness stands for in the book enables the pure exchange of souls symbolized in Daniel's marriage to both Mirah and Mordecai.

It is true that this union seems to have textuality at its heart, but that textuality rigorously excludes all that Eliot has previously meant by "art." For art, like money in this novel, is international, widely disseminated through modern printing, and bent on the creation of fungible, cosmopolitan selves. The Cabbala, on the other hand, is a set of exclusive, closely guarded and hand-copied esoteric texts, bent on the creation of a cumulative but nevertheless unique Jewish self. Indeed, Mordecai's way of disseminating his culture evinces a desire to dispense even with these texts. His teaching of little Jacob, for example, proceeds by "a sort of outpouring in the ear of the boy" of "a Hebrew poem of his own." Jacob cannot even understand the words, but Mordecai assures himself that "The boy will get them engraved within him . . . it is a way of printing" (532–33). Mordecai may believe that this kind of "printing" will one day influence Jacob, but as Eliot would be the first to point out, this activity has nothing to do with authorship. No one is culpable for it.

What should we make of this repudiation of the realm of exchange deep enough to undermine even the exchanges of a cosmopolitan culture in which Eliot herself was immersed? We should first place it within a general reflux away from internationalism in England. Imperial competition, the loss of London's power as the undisputed center of international finance, and various other difficulties in international relations were building toward a new mood of nostalgic nationalism. In its own very tangential way, through the link of Jewish rather than English nationalism, the novel connects with all this and takes the necessary step beyond Arnoldian internationalism.

Daniel Deronda's achievement, though, certainly does not lie in its expression of renewed nationalistic spirit. It is the problem much more than the solution that we find compelling in this novel, the creation of a self-sustaining anxiety. And intricate investigation of the problem seems to refer to Eliot's particular experiences in the realm of exchange. Here, of course, one can only speculate, but these reflections on her career made at its close, when her anxieties had perhaps begun to subside, might give us new insights into Eliot's fears of authorship. Again, these do not include a fear of writing or any anxiety about handling pens. Rather, they center around the relationship between her public, authorial identity, her pseudonym George Eliot, and her private identity, the ambiguous Marian Evans Lewes. It must be remembered that the impropriety of the latter is what led to the adoption of the former. "George Eliot," as Ruby Redinger has amply demonstrated, was not just an enabling fictional masculine identity but was for many years a serious screen to disguise the author's identity. For it was feared, by Lewes, Eliot, and her publishers, that no one would buy the books of the scandalous Marian Evans.[21] Indeed, Eliot's great anxiety about how much she would make from her books seems entirely determined by the illicitness of her relationship to George Henry Lewes. Eliot alone of all Victorian authors felt as a constant reality the interchangeability, the equivalence of difference, between prostitution and authorship. For as Bracebridge Hemyng pointed out in his 1861 study of prostitution, there were two kinds of prostitutes: women who traded their services for the money of many men, and women who were privately kept, without benefit of marriage, by one man.[22]

This reflection gives a new meaning to that perhaps apocryphal account of what the name "Eliot" stands for: "To L. I owe it."[23]

The name might be a veritable I.O.U., a recognition of indebtedness as much as a statement of gratitude, and a promissory note for future exchanges. With Eliot's authorship she purchased her status as something other than a whore. What she denied in her private designation, Marian Evans Lewes, she coyly admits in her public designation: I am not married to this man; I owe him money or I am his concubine. In May of 1880, she married John Cross, and George Eliot, author, and Marian Evans Lewes, scandalous woman, went out of existence in the same instant.

NOTES

1. Sandra M. Gilbert and Susan Gubar, *The Madwoman in the Attic* (New Haven: Yale University Press, 1979).
2. F. D. Harvey, "Literacy in the Athenian Democracy," *Revue des Etudes Grecques* 79 (1966): 621. Also, Susan G. Cole, "Could Greek Women Read and Write?" *Women's Studies* 8 (1981): 137, 155. Both critics cite Menander, frag. 702k:
   Teach a woman letters? A terrible mistake!
   —Like feeding extra venom to a horrifying snake.
Cole also draws a connection between prostitution and reading and writing (p. 143). Moreover, Charles Segal claims, primarily on the basis of Sophocles' *Trachiniae* and Euripides' *Hippolytus,* that there is a general Greek suspicion of writing that associates it with trickery, concealed love, and female desire. Segal argues that there is a tendency in Greek literature to associate writing with the hidden, dangerous, interior space of female desire, "a duplicitous silent speaking that can subvert the authority of king and father. As a concentrated form of seduction and persuasion, such 'female' writing is doubly a threat to the masculine ideal of straightforward talk and forthright action" ("Greek Tragedy: Writing, Truth, and the Representation of the Self," in *Mnemai: Classical Studies in Memory of Karl K. Hudley,* ed. Harold J. Evjen [Chico, Calif.: Scholars Press, 1984], pp. 56–57).
3. This discussion is based on Marc Shell's *The Economy of Literature* (Baltimore: Johns Hopkins University Press, 1978), pp. 91–102.
4. I am indebted to Professor Thomas Laqueur of the University of California, Berkeley, History Department, who directed me to several

ancient texts on the infertility of women whose intercourse is too frequent and too passionate. The infertility of prostitutes is, for example, cited by Lucretius as an instance of the general rule that excessive sexual activity leaves women barren. See *The Nature of the Universe* (London: Penguin Books, 1970), p. 170.

5. W. M. Thackeray, "Les Mystères de Paris (The Mysteries of Paris), par Eugène Sue. Thieves' Literature of France," repr. in Helga Grubitzsch, *Materialien zur Kritik des Feuilleton-Romans* (Wiesbaden: Akademische Verlagsgesellschaft Athenaion, 1977), p. 247.

6. George Eliot, "Silly Novels by Lady Novelists," *Westminster Review* N.S. 10 (1856): 461.

7. Ibid., p. 448.

8. "Authorship," *Leaves from a Notebook: The Works of George Eliot,* vol. 8 (New York: Nottingham Society, n.d.), pp. 209–10.

9. Ibid., p. 211.

10. See, for example, "The Too-Ready Writer," who, with "too much interest at his back," has not even a perception that can truly be called his. Despite his complete lack of productive capacity, however, the too-ready writer, like the usurer, manages to turn his real indebtedness to the intellectual labor of others to his credit. "You perceive," sneers the essayist, "how proud he is of not being indebted to any writer: even with the dead he is on the creditor's side, for he is doing them the service of letting the world know what they meant better than [they] . . . themselves had any means of doing." *The Impressions of Theophrastus Such: The Works of George Eliot,* vol. 8 (New York: Nottingham Society, n.d.), p. 118.

11. *Theophrastus Such,* p. 189.

12. "Authorship," p. 211.

13. *Theophrastus Such,* pp. 88–89.

14. George Eliot, *Daniel Deronda,* ed. and intro. Barbara Hardy (repr., Baltimore: Penguin Books, 1970), p. 48. All subsequent references to this novel are to this edition and are cited parenthetically in the text by page number.

15. "Women Artists," *Westminster Review* N.S. 14 (1858): 164.

16. George Henry Lewes, *On Actors and the Art of Acting* (Leipzig: B. Tachnitz, 1875), repr. in *Literary Criticism of George Henry Lewes,* ed. Alice Kaminsky (Lincoln: University of Nebraska Press, 1964), p. 112.

17. Ibid.

18. *Theophrastus Such,* p. 157.

19. Matthew Arnold, *Culture and Anarchy,* ed. R. H. Super (Ann Arbor: University of Michigan Press, 1965), pp. 145–46.

20. *Theophrastus Such,* p. 149.

21. Ruby V. Redinger, *George Eliot: The Emergent Self* (New York: Alfred A. Knopf, 1975), pp. 391–400.

22. Bracebridge Hemyng, *Those Who Will Not Work,* companion vol. to Henry Mayhew's *London Labour and the London Poor* (London: Charles Griffin & Co., 1861), p. 213.

23. It cannot be said that Eliot was conscious of the "I-O-Lewes" nature of the name she chose. In his *Life of George Eliot* (New York: Thomas P. Crowell & Co., 1904), J. W. Cross says only, "I may mention here that my wife told me the reason she fixed on this name was that George was Mr. Lewes's Christian name, and Eliot was a good mouth-filling, easily pronounced word" (p. 219). Blanche Colton Williams offers no attribution when she says in *George Eliot* (New York: Macmillan Co., 1936), " 'George' she borrowed from Lewes. 'To L—I owe it' gave her 'Eliot,' which, however, was explained simply as 'a good mouth-filling word' " (pp. 131–32). But even if we decide that the interpretation of the name is entirely Williams's speculation, we are still left with the novelist's own very revealing explanation, which might have been the inspiration for Blanche Williams's interpretation. For to say that "Eliot" is a "good, mouth-filling word" is to remind us again that her identity as novelist is what saves her from the status of prostitute implied by financial dependence on Lewes.

 *Gillian Beer*

Origins and Oblivion
in Victorian Narrative

Forgetfulness is categorized as a malfunction of memory, and yet forgetting is our commonest experience. We do not remember great tracts of life, great tracts of narrative. Of its nature, what has been forgotten is not available to be discussed. Remembering is achievement—and memory is prized as we prize all human achievement, with a sense of the exceptional. A summary example of how acceptable is memory, how unacceptable forgetting, is that in working on this project I found it impossible to gain access to material in catalogues except by looking under memory: *forgetting* (except in the clinical intensification of amnesia), and even *oblivion,* were not available as subsections.[1] Forgetting is the habitual activity of each human being; oblivion covers all that has been forgotten. We all ride, largely unperturbed, what Shakespeare in *Richard III* called "the swallowing Gulfe of dark Forgetfulnesse, and deepe Oblivion" (act 3, scene 7). But there are times when the act of forgetting becomes crisis and the recognition of oblivion becomes threatening to a community. One such time was the end of the sixteenth century in England, another was the Victorian period.

In this essay I suggest connections between the ordinary act of ceasing to remember and deep anxieties about the extent of oblivion, the remoteness and unreclaimableness of origins, in Victorian creativity. I want to consider how and why some Victorian narratives resist or dwell upon the dissolution of record, and so to study an intersection between general reading-process and a particular historical period.

It is not surprising that forgetting and oblivion are frequently seen as antagonists within literature: a common great theme has been the heroic task of the poet who makes things last by writing them. However, it may be an unobserved professional deformation that as critics we tend to identify forgetting with inefficient reading and fail to notice how important in our experience of a fiction is the dissolution in memory of the specificity of the text. We remember (or pretend to remember) the totality of a narrative and so misread its passing. We dwell on particular passages with intense semantic attention, and we triumphantly recall the names of minor characters. But long narrative must either accept or combat the reader's constant forgetting. Many early novelists had few qualms about dissolution.

The multiplot form of many of the greatest Victorian fictions, particularly those of Dickens, Thackeray, and George Eliot, makes it difficult for the reader to remember all that passes by.[2] In Hardy, that difficulty becomes the mainspring of narrative meaning. I do not propose in this short paper (nor am I qualified) to enter the controversy among experimental psychologists as to whether all memory is stored (even though some is unusable) or whether most experiences pass through us and are irretrievably lost. In any case, the loss of individual memory was not the only form of the problem that beset Victorian writers. They were made enforcedly aware that life had been going on for millions of years before human memory existed: no memory of that state was possible; life and story did not require the human race. In such a situation, human beings' imaginative zeal in "decipherment," what Richard Owen and others called "the writing on the rocks," gave an entry into the prehuman past for human consciousness.[3] Another point of entry was what W. B. Carpenter, Aeneas Sweetland Dallas, and, later, Freud, thought of as the possibility that "involuntary, unconscious thought" harbored traces of existence prior to the individual's history and continuous with the extreme and infinitely remote emergence of humankind.[4]

Aeneas Sweetland Dallas, in the 1860s, conceives imagination as a "function" rather than a faculty, a function of what he calls "the Hidden Soul" or "unconscious" with its "perpetual magic of reminiscence hidden from our conscious life." And, in Derridean style, he writes that "imagination . . . is only a name for the free, unconscious play of thought. But the mind in free play works more as a whole than in conscious and voluntary effort."[5] Dallas's emphasis on imagination as an expression of the "involuntary and unconscious" mind accords with Walter Benjamin's description of Proust's acts of memory: "Is not the involuntary recollection, Proust's *mémoire involontaire,* much closer to forgetting than what is usually called memory? . . . When we awake each morning, we hold in our hands, usually weakly and loosely, but a few fringes of the tapestry of lived life, as loomed for us by forgetting. However, with our purposeful activity and, even more, our purposive remembering each day unravels the web and ornaments of forgetting." Benjamin's praise of forgetting, like his praise of boredom in "The Storyteller," has in it a grave and conscious reversal of our expectations. In "The Storyteller" he remarks, "There is nothing that commends a story to memory more effectively than that chaste compactness which precludes psychological analysis."[6] Victorian fiction, with its emphasis on multiplicity and arboreal form combined with psychological analysis, might seem at the opposite pole from such storytelling: copiousness, and hyperproductivity invite selection not complete recall.

My project does not use the metaphor of "background," with literature as the foreground and all other writing as a system of clues that will give access to literary experience. Rather, I want to examine creative narratives such as those of the geologist Sir Charles Lyell, Darwin, or the philologist Max Müller, and Winwood Reade, *alongside* Victorian works of fiction. I have argued elsewhere that the process of interchange of metaphors and concepts between fields is at its most active "in areas of unresolved conflict or problem" and that "the function of transposition may be as much to disguise as to lay bare."[7] It is in the spirit of that observation that I analyze the means writers used to control a newly intensified sense of evanescence associated with concepts of geological time, of extinction, and of irreversible and random genetic mutation. Each of these diminished the claims of memory. Oblivion is prospective as well as past, universal as well as individual. Both fear of the sun's cooling, as well as the new study of prehistory, play a part in the hazards of Victorian experience and in the encoding of that experience in fiction. It is to modernist and postmodernist narrative that we turn for the topic of forgetting, the emphasis on fissure, palimpsest, and faulture. But it is within Victorian written culture that we find the incentives—intellectual and emotional—toward that interrupted organization.

In some recent postmodernist fiction, forgetting has emerged both as topic and as remarked process in the reader's activity. In *One Hundred Years of Solitude* Gabriel Garcia Marquez describes the insomnia plague and the forgotten massacre, and at the same time confuses throughout the book the reader's notation of events and time by reusing names repeatedly for different individuals. Milan Kundera in *The Book of Laughter and Forgetting* signals the topic in his title and illustrates it in the episodes (and the episodic structure) of the book. Malcolm Bradbury in *The History Man* sets up a moralized tension between the postcausal immediacy of present-tense narrative, which figures the hero's irresponsible revolutionism, and the counterweight of forgotten history. At the end of the book we as readers are made to discover our own collusion with Howard. Like him, and encouraged by the book's organization, we have forgotten his wife, Barbara, who plays no part in the work's latter phases but reemerges in the final scene to cut her wrist: an act of suicide that admonishes the reader of the connection between guilt, failure, and forgetting. Forgetting has become associated in our narratives with guilt and trauma. Freud's moral struggle was to restore memories and by such recuperation to make them part of accountable consciousness. Since Freud, individuals' acts of forgetting are interpreted as purposeful, rather than as part of a general process of evanescence.

Though a recognition of strained memory has become topical,

readers habitually allow narrative language and sometimes narrative sequence to dissolve, unhampered by any insistence on retention, unless the text persistently prompts them to recall and store. For example, one of the pleasures of picaresque fiction is the reader's license to discard narrative, just as the hero sloughs off experience. Many Victorian novelists set up a creative problem for themselves and their readers by combining the amplitude and arboreal form of their large narratives with an increasing insistence on the moral duty to recall and connect. Elizabeth Ermarth wittily condenses the question: "In all realistic novels one of the chief moral problems characters face is that of making proper connections, literally by marriage, and figuratively by sustained increase of conscious grasp. The power to accomplish that is often associated with memory."[8] In Victorian multiplot novels the reader, even more than the characters, is required to recognize his or her own activity of remembering and to value it. We are made to feel responsible for sustaining memory and are put on our guard against natural forgetting. Such insistence on remembering, as Wolfgang Iser points out in *The Act of Reading,* may produce satiety. The "consensual" novel (Ermarth's term) seeks to offer a full and single understanding of the whole and in particular to encompass its own beginning and ending. That naturalization of beginning and ending draws on the ontogenetic model of the life cycle. Consider, then, the disturbances implicit in scientific findings that suggested that the model of the single life cycle could not be extended to describe the natural order and its history, and that narrative acts had no necessary coherence with the time patterns of the material world.

Human memory, even at its most extended, is not coincident with the past. The living world existed previous to the human race, outside language: it can be brought within language and narrative only by the deciphering of traces and fragments, the assemblage of record. Prehistory was a new study, and a new imagination, in the mid-nineteenth century. "Real events" were the business of the Victorian novelist as well as of the natural historian, and it may be that we should see the Victorian insistence on the "real" as in some measure a response to the loss of a close-knit beginning and ending in the natural world. No longer held in by the Mosaic time order, that history became mosaic of another sort, a piecing together of subsets into an interpretable picture. Words like *traces* and *decipherment* become central to geology, evolutionary theory, and fictional narrative at this time. Interpretation was the only assurance. So Lyell alludes to Barthold Georg Niebuhr's achievements in historiography to illuminate the importance of geological researches: "As we explore this magnificent field of enquiry, the sentiment of a great historian of our times may continually be present to our minds, that 'he who calls what has vanished back again into being, enjoys a bliss like that of creating.' " Near the outset of *Principles of Geology,* Lyell quotes the geologist James Hutton, whose work in *A System of the Earth* (1785) had undermined the testimony of "granitic writing" and decipherment.

> No small sensation was excited when Hutton seemed, with unhallowed hand, desirous to erase characters already regarded by many as sacred. "In the economy of the world," said the Scotch geologist, "I can find no traces of a beginning, no prospect of an end"; a declaration the more startling when coupled with the doctrine, that all past ages on the globe had been brought about by the slow agency of existing causes. The imagination was first fatigued and overpowered by endeavouring to conceive the immensity of time required for the annihilation of whole continents by so insensible a process; and when the thoughts had wandered through these interminable periods, no resting-place was assigned in the remotest distance. [9]

Hutton asserted that geology had nothing to do "with the origin of things." An unspoken, and unwritten—because humanly unobserved—world precedes us, of which Huxley said "the question of the moral government of such a world could no more be asked than we could reasonably seek for moral purpose in a kaleidoscope." [10] Macherey, in *Towards a Theory of Literary Production,* has reminded us that the idea of an origin is an appeal to bounds, a means of staying the slide into oblivion, and—in his analysis—a way of giving authority to bourgeois hegemony. The questioning of historical origins and of a nameable originator may give some of the anxious zest to the Victorian insistence on causality. Certainly, Hutton's definition of a world in which there are "no traces of a beginning, no prospect of an end" is a highly inconvenient shape for fiction—particularly for fiction that wishes to lay claim to coherence with a representable order of society and a "real" material world.

The Victorians were made preternaturally sensitive to the processes of forgetting and to the extent of what has been forgotten. They were made aware also of the vigorous life that long preceded human memory. Their fascination with history is one response to that awareness—as well as an intensifying symptom. But history was preoccupied with power, and what evolutionary theory brought out in contrast was the thronging powerlessness of the individual organisms who were the medium of change. At the end of *Middlemarch* George Eliot celebrates the "incalculably diffusive" outcome of Dorothea's life and of other unrecounted lives and ends her "domestic epic" with a bare gradualism that just admits the possibility of improvement: "For the growing good of the world is partly dependent on unhistoric acts; and that things are not so ill with you and me as they might have been, is half owing to the forgotten numbers who lived faithfully a hidden life, and rest in unvisited tombs."[11] The "forgotten numbers" are the permitting medium of our present experience.

The insistence on displacing the experience of the individual life cycle into that of the society or species is so familiar to us that we rarely, too rarely perhaps, examine it. The vacillation between ontogeny and phylogeny has been the most powerful new metaphor of the past hundred years, affecting areas as diverse as race history and musicology. The growth of the single organism was an ancient metaphor; the growth of species and the paralleling of the two was new. One means by which the Victorians imaginatively healed their sense of the enormity of oblivion was by the concepts of "recapitulation" and "survivals": the embryo "recapitulates" the phases of evolutionary development, while remote tribes are "survivals" from the "childhood of man." Freud openly used the vacillation between individual organism and species history in the case of Dr. Schreber (1911) and *Totem and Taboo* (1913), and he continued to hold this view through the 1930s, as demonstrated in *Moses and Monotheism*. The past precedes human memory and is irrecoverable, except by conjoining ontogeny and phylogeny. Freud uses this essentially Victorian conjunction in the postscript to "Notes on a Case of Paranoia":

> The mythopoeic forces of mankind are not extinct, but . . . to this very day they give rise in the neuroses to the same psychical products as in the remotest past ages. . . . I am of opinion that the time will soon be ripe for us to make an extension of a thesis which has long been asserted by psychoanalysts, and to complete what has hitherto had only an individual and ontogenetic application by the addition of its anthropological counterpart, which is to be conceived phylogenetically. "In dreams and in neuroses" our thesis has run, "we come once more upon the child and the peculiarities which characterize his modes of thought and his emotional life." "And we come upon the savage too," we may now add, "upon the primitive man, as he stands revealed to us in the light of the researches of archaeology and ethnology." [12]

Sir Charles Lyell, whose *Principles of Geology*, stretched time backward an unknown and irrecoverable extent, emphasized the differing narrative properties of his account of the world and the accounts of previous geologists.

> We often behold, at one glance, the effects of causes which have acted at times incalculably remote, and yet there may be no striking circumstances to make the occurrence of a great chasm in the chronological series of Nature's archives. In the vast interval of time which may really have elapsed between the results of operations thus compared, the physical condition of the earth may, by slow and insensible modifications, have become entirely altered; one or more races of organic beings may have passed away, and yet have left behind, in the particular region under contemplation, no trace of their existence. [13]

The short span of time previously allowed to events has implied, said Lyell, a narrative of catastrophe and revolution, of upheaval and reversal, a magical or nightmare romance:

> How fatal every error as to the quantity of time must prove to the introduction of rational views concerning the state of things in former ages, may be conceived by supposing the annals of the civil and military transactions of a great nation to be perused under the impression that they occurred in a period of one hundred instead of two thousand years. Such a portion of history would immediately assume the air of a romance; the events would seem devoid of credibility, and inconsistent with the present course of human affairs. A crowd of incidents would follow each other in quick succession. Armies and fleets would appear to be assembled only to be destroyed, and cities built merely to fall in ruins. There would be the most violent transitions from foreign or intestine war to periods of profound peace, and the works effected during the years of disorder or tranquility would appear alike superhuman in magnitude. He who should study the monuments of the natural world under the influence of a similar infatuation, must draw a no less exaggerated picture of the energy and violence of causes. [14]

Previous geologists were like the seven sleepers who awoke to a transformed world, unaware of their immense slumbers. The reach of time in Lyell's narrative is turned into a means of comfort by suggesting continuity and slight change as the agencies of transformation.

But that quiet world of slippage, erosion, and dead forms is disturbed again by Robert Chambers in *Vestiges of the Natural History of Creation* (1844) and Charles Darwin in *Of the Origin of Species by Means of Natural Selection, of the Preservation of Favoured Races in the Struggle for Life* (1859). The full title of Darwin's work brings out the ideological contrast between his arguments and those of Chambers. For Chambers, what is left in the world is "vestiges"—fragmentary records of a primordial creation—and "natural history" is the storying of creation, arranging it in a narrative sequence that will not question the initiating act. Darwin, on the other hand, substitutes process for initiation, place, or person. "Of the Origin . . . by Means of":

originating is no longer to be identified with an originator, or
with a place of origin. It would be going too far to describe Darwin's project as "free-play without origins" as Derrida describes
the nature of poetry, but it is a significant move away from the
idea of history and of natural history as a tracking back to a
recoverable origin. Darwin develops Lyell's metaphor of the
material world as language, or as a Borgesian, language-ridden
history of language, itself written in an alien tongue.

> For my part, following out Lyell's metaphor, I look at the natural
> geological record, as a history of the world imperfectly kept, and
> written in a changing dialect; of this history we possess the last volume
> alone, relating only to two or three countries. Of this volume, only here
> and there a short chapter has been preserved; and of each page, only
> here and there a few lines. Each word of the slowly-changing language, in
> which the history is supposed to be written, being more or less different
> in the interrupted succession of chapters, may represent the apparently
> abruptly changed forms of life, entombed in our consecutive, but
> widely separated formations. [15]

The account of forgotten worlds that Lyell and Darwin provided relied not upon catastrophe but upon an immense elonga-
tion of time and on a recognition of how recent—and how frail—
was the hold of the human within the natural order. Lyell
thought it quite probable that the human race would die out
again and the world revert to earlier states. Darwin emphasized
that few if any current species forms would carry forward into
the prolonged future. Not only individuals but whole species
take part in the immense and irrecoverable process of forgetting
and of being forgotten. Lyell's and Darwin's work raised the
problem of how to sustain a narrative form that would satisfy
the demand for coherence while acknowledging evanescence.

Hayden White in "The Narrativization of Real Events" writes:
"I assume we agree that narrativization is what Fredric Jameson
calls 'the central function or instance of the human mind' or a
form of human comprehension that is productive of meaning by
its imposition of a certain formal coherence on a virtual chaos

of 'events' which in themselves (or as given to perception) cannot be said to possess any particular form at all, much less the kind that we associate with 'stories.' The question is with what *kind of meaning* does storying endow these events which are the products of human agency in the past and which we call 'historical events.' " Making an important distinction, White goes on to remark that there is no sense in speaking of "events per se," only "events under description."[16] White writes of the "storying" of events that are the products of human agency. The Victorians were faced also with the problem of "storying" events prior to the human and regardless of the human—and of making sense of the human story in this enlarged field. Is the forgotten period simply a repetition of what is now enacted, or is it increasingly different, more alien, less retrievable? Is the present therefore less universal than it has seemed, more purely local and passing also? Was there a particular historical problem for the Victorians in relation to the project of realism? Could realism itself be said to emerge from a dismayed recognition of the extensiveness of oblivion, the manifold and unremitting activities of forgetting?

Darwinian theory brings into question the value of memory. It highlights the extent of our inevitable ignorance of the lived past, both our own past and that of the physical order of the world. It denies, in its earlier stages, the inscribing of experience as inherited characteristics. It emphasizes "luck" as opposed to "cunning," to use Samuel Butler's later pair of contraries. It refuses both chance and necessity and—with Lyell—emphasizes the inadequacy of our perspective as observers. It also prepares for a recovery of the human position through the idea of the unconscious. But for Lyell, for Darwin, and for Huxley, the unconscious was not the guardian of prior memories, but rather a separate domain, relating to the earth's movements, and to "natural" instead of "artificial" selection, genetic as opposed to reasoned continuity.[17]

In Hardy's small, profound poem, "Heredity," we hear the menace and promise of impersonal genetic continuity:

I am the family face;
Flesh perishes, I live on,
Projecting trait and trace
Through times to times anon,
And leaping from place to place
Over oblivion. [18]

That poem, with its emphasis on haphazard and partial genetic survival (a survival that obliterates individual significance), was written toward the end of a period that had almost intolerably extended the awareness of "oblivion."

"History" becomes "natural history," with the profoundly equivocal meaning that "natural" bears at this period: "natural history," "natural theology," "Natural Selection." The ironic relationships among these terms pivot upon their common element "natural." Human beings are both newly, and completely, part of the natural order—in evolutionary theory they are not set apart from other species. Yet they must also become the chroniclers of tracts of time in which they had no place: "before the lowest Silurian stratum was deposited, long periods elapsed . . . during these vast, yet quite unknown, periods of time, *the world swarmed with living creatures*" (emphasis added). That perception Darwin saw as crucial to this theory, indisputable yet beyond memorial. He, like Lyell, commented on the difficulty of believing in the vastness of time and the tendency to close the gaps in the record. Darwin saw the narrative problem of recording such "vast intervals": "When we see the formations tabulated in written works, it is difficult to avoid believing that they are closely consecutive." Tabulation erases intermittence. The record is paltry in the extreme. "I have made these few remarks because it is highly important for us to gain some notion, however imperfect, of the lapse of years. During each of these years, over the whole world, the land and the water have been peopled by hosts of living forms. What an infinite number of generations, which the mind cannot grasp, must have succeeded each other in the long roll of years! Now turn to our richest geological museums, and what a paltry display we behold!"[19] In *Science and the Hebrew Tradition* Huxley later comments on the importance of the imperfection of the geological record: "This imperfection is a great fact, which must be taken into account in all our speculations, or we shall constantly be going wrong."[20]

Here we have possible incentives within the culture for the rise of the detective story, with its emphasis on lost clues, determined reading, recuperable losses, the deciphering of traces: a way of controlling the hermeneutic plethora, "the imposition of a certain formal coherence on a virtual chaos of 'events'" (Hayden White). Detective fiction is a form that draws the reader's attention to his or her own processes of forgetting and of inattention. It establishes a nameable origin for its action. It restores coherence at the price of amplitude, though as Frank Kermode observes: "Even in a detective story which has the maximum degree of specialised hermeneutic organisation, one can always find significant concentrations of interpretable material that has nothing to do with clues and solutions and that can, if we choose, be read rather than simply discarded, though propriety recommends the latter course."[21] These "significant concentrations of interpretable material" may be said to be the "hosts of living forms" redundant to story, history, or even explanation.

For Victorian writers, the detective or mystery story emerges as the form in which it remains satisfyingly possible to go back and rediscover the true initiation of a history. In such an organization we are assured that "the traces of the past [lie] deep—too deep to be effaced." Wilkie Collins here connects the imagery of geology and decipherment with that of subconscious memory and trauma. He emphasizes the survival of traces, not their obliteration. In such a plot truth-telling and interpretation are close to paranoia. Nothing is contingent, everything can be retraced to a single initiating source. In paranoid plot the loss of authentic origin makes the acts of decipherment and interpretation both

self-generating and self-consuming. Here, Hartright's monomania
is sane, but barely so: "I began to doubt whether my own facul-
ties were not in danger of losing their balance. It seemed almost
like a monomania to be tracing back everything strange that
happened, everything unexpected that was said, always to the
same hidden source and the same sinister influence."[22] Nothing
may be forgotten by the reader or the first-person narrator, since
all information is usable. Such fiction thrives on the guilt of
misinterpretation and the satisfaction of the single solution, an
austere reassembly of evidences.

In a world jostling with multiformity, fissured by incomplete
meaning, the dogged and dedicated search for the single solution, the recovered origin, becomes one pressing narrative response. The reader is both chastened and heartened, chastened
by his or her misclued memory, the tendency to retain what is
not needed and discard the unnoticed that was crucial. The
form of the detective story emphasizes the reader's attention to
his or her own reading process and, at the conclusion, makes
possible the satisfactory rereading of the past. For, in writing,
death is never absolute. By turning back the pages we retrieve
the earlier form. Obliteration is impossible: the traces never
give way. This is indeed a technical problem for detective story
writers, but also part of the synchronic pleasures that the form
offers. The rise of the detective story may have to do, I suggest,
with the Victorian anxiety about forgetting. Origins, within
detective narratives, are still figured as recoverable by means of
astute reading. But such reading is also transparently a fictive
act, devoted to a form that declares its elucidations to be
fictional.

In discussion of origins, the ontogenetic/phylogenetic/onto-
genetic interchange may help also to account for the insistent
search for parentage in Victorian fiction. Dianne F. Sadoff, in
Monsters of Affection, has offered a fascinating Freudian reading of the role of the father in Victorian novels and in the novelists' imaginations.[23] The individual's psychohistory, however, is

supplemented by shared perturbations, particularly communal perturbations such as the loss of congruity between human history and the history of the natural order. The insistence on the father, who is both an immediate and an uncertain origin, is a means of stabilizing the human record. The search for the mother, as in *Daniel Deronda,* shares the genetic recognition that W. R. Grove offered in his 1866 presidential address to the British Association for the Advancement of Science: "From the long continued conventional habit of tracing pedigrees through the male ancestor, we forget in talking of progenitors that each individual has a mother as well as a father, and there is no reason to suppose that he has in him less of the blood of the one than of the other."[24] Women are forgotten in the history of descent as they largely are in the historical record. In the new emphasis on genetic descent as the primary means of storying the past, it became necessary to recognize the generative power of the mother.

Without denying either the social or the psychosexual incentives for this topic, we may better understand the intensity of the theme if we measure it in relation to longer-spanning anxieties that preceded Darwin and were fed by Lyell and Chambers, among others. In Dickens's *Bleak House* the themes of lost parentage, of obliterated record or "traces" and the consternation of a lawsuit preoccupied with "pedigree" and with the descent of the great family are at last voided of content. Throughout this book it is the *effort* of memory that is the focus. Deciperment is the reader's task; writing is the scrivener's and the copyist's. The legal documents that are copied turn out to be burdened with Nothingness, just as the scrivener is Nobody— Nemo. Krook forgets nothing and can decipher nothing, only copy it. At the end of *Bleak House,* when the threatened apocalypse arrives, it takes the form of emptiness. The end of the lawsuit is the end of memory; there is no longer substance in the lawsuit, either of cash or meaning. The lawsuit "lapsed and melted away"; Richard can only "begin the world" in another world. The immense clutter of Dickens's creativity allows us to forget much as we read, while, increasingly, in his later work, Dickens introduces means of making us aware of our forgetfulness. In *Bleak House* he uses the multiple cluing of Tulkinghorn and Bucket and Guppy, with their different detective-story insistences, to revive and limit meaning. All these interlocking themes should be seen within the framework of Dickens alerting the reader by means of abrupt cross-setting of systems in the introductory paragraph of the book, a paragraph that looks back to prehistory and forward to the death of the sun.

> London. Michaelmas Term lately over, and the Lord Chancellor sitting in Lincoln's Inn Hall. Implacable November weather. As much mud in the streets, as if the waters had but newly retired from the face of the earth, and it would not be wonderful to meet a Megalosaurus, forty feet long or so, waddling like an elephantine lizard up Holborn Hill. Smoke lowering down from chimney-pots, making a soft black drizzle, with flakes of soot in it as big as full-grown snow-flakes—gone into mourning, one might imagine, for the death of the sun. [25]

J. Hillis Miller has drawn attention to the irreconcilable gaps between the two narrators' accounts in this novel, gaps caused in part because the narrators live in different tenses—one opened out toward imminent apocalypse in the dangerous present tense, one reaching back to an understanding of the historical past. [26] But the cross-setting of systems goes further than that. The paragraph just cited sets side by side the new and old versions of origins and apocalypse and offers them in playful synchrony: "waters newly retired," "Megalosaurus," "the death of the sun." Mosaic creation, evolutionary theory derived from Chambers, modern London with its street names, its particularity of local place, are all conjoined: a barely postdeluvian geology is set alongside soot like black snowflakes "gone into mourning . . . for the death of the sun." That allusion calls in still another Victorian anxiety: the new theory current since the physicist Hermann von Helmholtz's 1847 essay *Über die Erhaltung der Kraft,* which argued that the sun is gradually cooling and that the earth will become too cold for life.

Ten years after Dickens's novel, Max Müller offered his theory of myth in which metaphor figures as "a disease of language"— a disease brought about by forgetfulness and resulting in mythology. The lost relation between substantive first meaning and later etymological shift results, Müller argues, in false personification. In Müller's system all signification leads back toward the sun and the phenomena of weather, and to the fear of nonrecurrence. He claimed that primitive peoples feared that the sun would not rise again.[27] Frances Power Cobbe's *Darwinism in Morals* recounts a terrifying dream that goes deep into the current imagery of her culture: the loss of faith in *recurrence,* the loss of any assurance of "eternal return," the recognition that oblivion is not only the matter of the past but of the future. We have seen already a slight reference to "the death of the sun" in Dickens. By the 1870s it has begun to trouble dreams by night:

I dreamed that I was standing on a certain broad grassy space in the park of my old home. It was totally dark, but I was sure that I was in the midst of an immense crowd. We were all gazing upward into the murky sky and a sense of some fearful calamity was over us, so that no one spoke aloud. Suddenly overhead appeared through a rift in the black heavens, a branch of stars which I recognised as the belt and sword of Orion. Then went forth a cry of despair from all our hearts! We knew, though no one said it, that these stars proved it was not a cloud or mist which, as we had somehow believed, was causing the darkness. No; the air was clear; it was high noon, and *the sun had not risen!* That was the tremendous reason why we beheld the skies. The sun would never rise again![28]

Max Müller's solar myth was so powerful because it gave expression to covert dreads then current: it cast itself as past inquiry, but expressed current fears. In Freud's "Notes on a Case of Paranoia," Dr. Schreber's "delusional privilege" will be the power to look directly at the sun, which in Freud's analysis signifies the father. Solar myth becomes parental myth.

In *Vestiges* Chambers describes memory as "that handmaid of intellect, without which there could be no accumulation of mental capital, but an universal and continual infancy."[29] The mixture of economic and ontogenetic metaphors—capital and infancy—is striking here. In his most anticapitalist novel, *Little Dorrit,* Dickens shows the appalling effects of memory that is clung to. Mrs. Clennam, with her reading of the motto on her husband's watch "Do Not Forget," stultifies her own life and those of others. The vengeful repetitiveness of her memory means that no growth or change is possible. She is literally seized by the force of her resentment, which constantly replays the past. Her crazed clinging to the capital sum of memory (her husband's love affair) and her closed economic and emotional system feed everything back into the one originating event. " 'Do Not Forget'. It spoke to me like a voice from an angry cloud. Do not forget the deadly sin, do not forget the appointed discovery, do not forget the appointed suffering. I did not forget."[30] Mrs. Clennam's is an extreme of monomaniac memory that enforces the idea of the single origin. Through *Little Dorrit* Dickens suggests connections between the circulation or piling up of money and the circulation or piling up of memory. Forgetting and letting go prove to be the most difficult of achievements, as we see in the history of Dorrit himself.

These combined dreads and "delusional privileges" are taken into Hardy's imagination and powerfully share in his fictional process, particularly in *Tess of the D'Urbervilles,* with its solar myths of Stonehenge and the Druids and Tess's alliance to the sun. In Hardy people may long to be forgotten, not remembered. So Tess's lament opens, "I would that folk forgot me quite," and ends:

I cannot bear my fate as writ,
I'd have my life unbe;
Would turn my memory to a blot,

Make every relic of me rot,
My doings be as they were not,
And gone all trace of me![31]

The combination of the discourses of writing ("blot" and
"trace") and of fossil evidence ("rot" and "trace") lightly bears
the weight of Victorian awareness of slight signs as the only
surviving evidence of lives that can still never be reknown.

In Hardy we find a writer who was willing to encounter the
activity of forgetting, to let go origins, and to encompass
oblivion—with pain certainly, but without panic. He records
that some times are "silent beyond the possibility of echo." He
allows his reader the fullest experience of discovering, of losing,
and of forgetting, and parallels the profound insights of the
evolutionary theorists. A great number of forms, argues Darwin,
have been "utterly lost." Relations between current forms and
"their ancient and unknown progenitor" may be tracked, but
the progenitor must remain unknown. "Not one living species
will transmit its unaltered likeness to a distant futurity. And of
the species now living, very few will transmit progeny of any
kind to a far distant futurity."[32] Darwinian record, in *The Origin
of Species,* is a record of descent and dispersal, not of learning
or memory.

Storying in Hardy is *itself* tragic process; happiness lies only
in the constellated moments of sense experience. Much Victorian
narrative, as opposed to modernist and postmodernist narrative,
presents itself as a sufficient act of remembering, and of forgetting. Writing parallels record and memory, reading participates in that metamemory immediately created: but reading
participates, too, in the desuetude of memory, the ebbing of the
experienced instant. Hardy allows the reader to have, to lose,
and then to forget the loss—sometimes through the trauma of a
plot's extremity, sometimes through the gentler hazard of narrative extension. As readers we glimpse in Hardy's writing lives
unrecorded, this year's installment of ephemeral being. Yet
memory is also granted a heroic meaning, sustained past the end

of the narrative, and not yet yielding to our oblivion. Marty South remembers Winterborne like the meaning of a knoll, a dip, a rise.

At the end of Hardy's *The Mayor of Casterbridge* Michael Henchard retreats into a countryside where nothing is forgotten, though only because nothing of human meaning has happened there between primeval times and now: "that ancient country whose surface never had been stirred to a finger's depth, save by the scratching of rabbits, since brushed by the feet of the earliest tribes." Characteristically, for Hardy, memory takes its furthest reach from touch and architecture. The tumuli are the only trace of former ancestral human lives. The last item of Henchard's will is "that no man remember me"—a command that arrestingly negates itself.[33] His death is almost the sole event of that quiet country, but, as Hayden White reminds us, this is a question not of "events in themselves" but "events under description." Along-side Henchard's death we have the narrative description of the dwelling where his body lay. The architectural crumbling of materials is Hardy's characteristic enregisterment of the crumbling of narrative record. Forgotten lives, unrecorded beings, are hinted at in the description of natural materials built into dwellings and decaying back into nature: "The walls, built of kneaded clay originally faced with a trowel, had been worn by years of rain-washings to a lumpy crumbling surface, channelled and sunken from its plane, its grey rents held together here and there by a leafy strap of ivy which could scarce find substance enough for the purpose."[34] The clay is "kneaded," "faced with a trowel." Origins, as in other such passages in Hardy, discreetly move in the vocabulary, here subdued and curtailed to a moment of workmanlike activity, "originally faced with a trowel," which is succeeded by years of rain washing, and strapped by ivy. "Strap" again suggests the workman, but the ivy is vagrantly active according only to its own needs. Purpose gives way.

In *Tess of the D'Urbervilles*, kind (both cattle and humans) survive only in totally metamorphosed forms—cattle as a glossy post. At the Dairy, "long thatched sheds stretched round the enclosure, their slopes encrusted with vivid green moss, and their eaves supported by wooden posts rubbed to a glossy smoothness by the flanks of infinite cows and calves of bygone years, now passed to an oblivion almost inconceivable in its profundity." Or, as Darwin put it, the "hosts of living forms. . . . an infinite number of generations, which the mind cannot grasp" have vanished in their turn into unrecorded oblivion. On the next page Tess is reminded "that a family of some such name as yours in Blackmoor Vale came originally from these parts and that 'twere an old ancient race that had all but perished off the earth—though the new generations didn't know it."[35] Again "originally" sketches in a provisional beginning that serves to measure the distance into near-extinction.

Tess stands on the landscape "the hemmed expanse of verdant flatness, like a fly on a billiard-table of indefinite length, and of no more consequence to her surroundings than that fly."[36] Hardy draws here upon the imagery of Winwood Reade's *The Martyrdom of Man,* published in the early 1870s and frequently reprinted until the Second World War. Reade's was the most eloquent and popular Victorian response to the tragic implications of Darwinian evolutionary theory: "the earth resembles a picture, of which we, like insects which crawl upon its surface, can form but a faint and incoherent idea. . . . We belong to the minutiae of Nature, we are in her sight, as the raindrop of the sky; whether a man lives, or whether he dies, is . . . a matter of indifference to Nature. . . . Men . . . have no connection with Nature, except through the organism to which they belong." The pain of the individual is both absolute and without major consequence. In response to the developmental "progressive" reading of man's history, Reade writes bleakly: "Pain is not less pain because it is useful; murder is not less murder because it is conducive to development. . . . Those who believe in a God of Love must close their eyes to the phenomena of life, or garble the universe to suit their theory."[37] Reade, writing his strange history of the world, broods on the lost and irrecoverable nature of the past and on the constant stress between the individual's intense experience of life and the failure of this individual meaning to survive. Of all the nonfictional narratives of the time, Reade's comes closest to Hardy's creative contradictions.

Hardy's novels are haunted by Darwin's "forgotten multitudes"; through "unknown ages" the world "has swarmed with living creatures," denizens of the natural order that include cows, plants, birds, men and women, hairy caterpillars. The sensuousness of our imagining of this unpurposed multitude is posed painfully against the individual purposiveness of trilobites or men: "the creature had had a body to save, as he himself had now"—so thinks Knight, in Hardy's *A Pair of Blue Eyes,* in kinship with the fossil trilobite whose eyes stare at him from the cliff face as he expects to fall.[38] The arbitrariness of record puzzled Darwin and Huxley. They insisted on the need to preserve awareness of incompleteness and fissured history, the inadequacy of traces, as in itself important evidence: "The whole world, the land and the water have been peopled by hosts of living forms. . . . Now turn to our richest geological museums, and what a paltry display we behold." Typically, with the word "peopled," Darwin indicates the kinship of all those lived and lost lives, lives fully lived and fully forgotten. Evidence and record are both profoundly inadequate: "What an infinite number of generations, which the mind cannot grasp, must have succeeded each other in the long roll of years!"[39]

"The mind cannot grasp" what has been forgotten. The world is always full. Memory fills up the extent of life available to it and makes us forget what lies beyond. Hardy keeps faith with oblivion, but disturbs our sense of completeness by the allusive system that anthropomorphically glimpses past and other states of being. Through geology, prehistory, the extension of the past, the insistence in evolutionary ideas on change and loss of nameable origins, the forgetting and deforming of meaning in language, the debilitating of memory as an agent of transformation and control in Darwinian theory—through all these factors, together with a common insistence on growth, the Victorians were made to be aware of how much was irretrievably forgotten, and to set great store by those signs and traces, those acts of decipherment that relieved oblivion and reconstituted themselves as origins.

NOTES

1. Compare Mircea Eliade, *Myth and Reality* (New York: Harper & Row, 1963), p. 136: "It seems as if Western culture were making a prodigious effort of historiographic *anamnesis* . . . this *anamnesis* continues the religious evaluation of memory and forgetfulness."

2. This leads Northrop Frye to write of Dickens's late novels as "anti-narratives" (*The Secular Scripture* [Cambridge, Mass.: Harvard University Press, 1976], p. 40).

3. For example, Richard Owen, address to the British Association for the Advancement of Science, 1858: "Yet, during all those æras that have passed since the Cambrian rocks were deposited which bear the impressed record of Creative power, as it was then manifested, we know, through the interpreters of these 'writings on stone,' that the earth was vivified by the sun's light and heat. . . . The earliest testimony of the living thing, whether shell, crust, or coral in the oldest fossiliferous rock, is at the same time proof that it died" (quoted in G. Basalla, W. Coleman, and R. Kargon, eds., *Victorian Science* [Garden City, N.Y.: Doubleday & Co., 1970], p. 313). Note the biblical suggestion of tablets, "the impressed record of Creative power," and "testimony."

4. Aeneas Sweetland Dallas, *The Gay Science* (London, 1866), 2: 110: "All pleasure has a tendency to forget itself, and there is no escape from the paradox that a large number of our joys, including some of the highest, scarcely, if ever, come into the range of consciousness." Frances Cobbe Power, in *Darwinism in Morals* (London, 1872), p. 307, summarizes the then-current terms as "Latent Thought," "Preconscious Activity of the Soul," and "Unconscious Cerebration." See also Samuel Butler, *Unconscious Memory* (London, 1880).

5. Dallas, *Gay Science* 1:210, 305.

6. Walter Benjamin, "The Image of Proust," in *Illuminations* (London: Fontana/Collins, 1973), p. 204; "The Storyteller," in ibid., p. 91.

7. Gillian Beer, "Anxiety and Interchange: *Daniel Deronda* and the Implications of Darwin's Writing," *Journal of the History of the Behavioral Sciences* 19 (1983): 31.

8. Elizabeth Ermarth, *Realism and Consensus in the English Novel* (Princeton, N.J.: Princeton University Press, 1983), p. 21.

9. Charles Lyell, *Principles of Geology; or, The Modern Changes of the Earth and Its Inhabitants,* 10th rev. ed. in 2 vols. (London, 1867), 1:89, 76. First published, 3 vols., 1830–33.

10. Thomas Henry Huxley, *Science and Christian Tradition* (London, 1894), p. 45.

11. George Eliot, *Middlemarch* (Harmondsworth: Penguin Books, 1965), p. 896.

12. Sigmund Freud, "Notes on a Case of Paranoia," *The Pelican Freud Library* (Harmondsworth: Penguin Books, 1979), 9:222-23.

13. Lyell, *Principles of Geology* 1:96.

14. Ibid., p. 94.

15. Jacques Derrida, *Writing and Difference,* trans. Alan Bass (Chicago: University of Chicago Press, 1978), p. 292; Charles Darwin, *On the Origin of Species* (1859; repr., Cambridge, Mass.: Harvard University Press, 1964), p. 310.

16. Hayden White, "The Narrativization of Real Events," *Critical Inquiry* 8 (1981): 795.

17. For a fuller discussion of these questions see my *Darwin's Plots: Evolutionary Narrative in Darwin, George Eliot, and Nineteenth-Century Fiction* (London: Routledge & Kegan Paul, 1983).

18. "Heredity," in *The Complete Poems of Thomas Hardy,* New Wessex Edition (London: Macmillan & Co., 1976), p. 434.

19. Darwin, *Origin of Species,* pp. 307, 287.

20. Thomas Henry Huxley, *Science and the Hebrew Tradition* (repr., New York: Greenwood Press, 1968), p. 85. Huxley follows these remarks by discussion and illustrations of the tracks of a species of enormous prehistoric creatures and the unsolved mystery of their disappearance (pp. 87–89).

21. Frank Kermode, "Secrets and Narrative Sequence," *Critical Inquiry* 7 (1980): 87.

22. Wilkie Collins, *The Woman in White,* ed. Harvey Sucksmith, The World's Classics (Oxford: Oxford University Press, 1975), p. 69.

23. Dianne F. Sadoff, *Monsters of Affection: Dickens, Eliot, and Brontë on Fatherhood* (Baltimore: Johns Hopkins University Press, 1982).

24. Quoted in Basalla, Coleman, and Kargon, eds., *Victorian Science,* p. 346.

25. Charles Dickens, *Bleak House,* Authentic Edition (London, 1901), p. 1.

26. J. H. Miller in "Introduction" to Charles Dickens, *Bleak House* (Harmondsworth: Penguin Books, 1971).

27. Max Müller, *Lectures on the Science of Language,* series 1 and 2 (London, 1861, 1862).

28. Francis Power Cobbe, "Dreams as Illustrations of Unconscious Cerebration," *Macmillan's Magazine* 23 (April 1871): 515; repr. in Cobbe's *Darwinism in Morals.*

29. Robert Chambers, *Vestiges of the Natural History of Creation* (London, 1844; facsimile, New York: Humanities Press, 1969, with "Introduction" by Gavin de Beer), p. 342.

30. Charles Dickens, *Little Dorrit,* Authentic Edition (London, 1901), p. 740. The reader is guarded from any embroilment in Mrs. Clennam's memories. It is not until the end of the book that we hear her story. This work functions at the level of social and individual memory and forgetting, and I introduce it to delimit my argument, since I can read in it no trace of what I have called phylogenetic disturbance. Individualism is the work's scale as much as the value it sets against disorder. In this it differs from *Bleak House.*

31. *The Complete Poems of Thomas Hardy,* pp. 175, 177.

32. Darwin, *Origin of Species,* p. 344.

33. Thomas Hardy, *The Mayor of Casterbridge,* New Wessex Edition (London: Macmillan & Co., 1975), p. 353.

34. Ibid., p. 330.

35. Thomas Hardy, *Tess of the D'Urbervilles,* New Wessex Edition (London: Macmillan & Co., 1975), p. 133; Darwin, *Origin of Species,* p. 287; Hardy, *Tess,* p. 134.

36. Hardy, *Tess,* p. 136.

37. Winwood Reade, *The Martyrdom of Man* (repr., London: Rationalist Press Association, 1924), pp. 429, 428, 435.

38. Thomas Hardy, *A Pair of Blue Eyes,* New Wessex Edition (London: Macmillan & Co., 1976), p. 222.

39. Darwin, *Origin of Species,* p. 287.

Elaine Showalter

Syphilis, Sexuality, and the Fiction of the Fin de Siècle

If, as Susan Sontag has maintained in *Illness as Metaphor*, tuberculosis and cancer became the symbolic diseases of the nineteenth and twentieth centuries, syphilis was surely the symbolic disease of the fin de siècle. Suggesting the dread of sexual contamination during a period of gender crisis, the iconography of syphilis pervades English fiction at the turn of the century. While syphilis and syphilitic insanity constituted the repressed historical referents for the fantastic mode that dominates so much of late Victorian writing, male and female fantasies were very different. For fin-de-siècle women writers, lust was the most unforgivable of the sins of the fathers, and sexual disease was its punishment, a punishment unjustly shared by innocent women and children. By the 1890s the syphilitic male had become an arch-villain of feminist protest fiction, a carrier of contamination and madness, and a threat to the spiritual evolution of the human race. In men's writing of the period, however, women are the enemies, whether as the femmes fatales who lure men into sexual temptation only to destroy them, the frigid wives who drive them to the brothels, or the puritanical women novelists, readers, and reviewers who would emasculate their art. By the end of the century, the imaginative worlds of male and female writers had become radically separate, and the sexual struggle between men and women had a counterpart in a literary struggle over the future of fiction.

Why should syphilis have played so central a symbolic role in the fiction of the 1890s? Susan Sontag relates the efflorescence of metaphors of illness to moments when the disease in question is coming under some medical control, but remains frightening and mysterious.[1] Although syphilis was incurable until the twentieth century, the rates of the disease were actually beginning to decline in the 1890s, probably because of improved hygiene, after a period in which alarm over the high incidence of syphilis among soldiers and sailors had led to control of prostitution by the English government in the controversial Contagious Diseases Acts of 1864-1886.[2] Culturally, moreover, the discourse on syphilis was part of what Foucault sees as the post-Darwinian theory of degenerescence, part of the new technologies of sex that opened up the domain of social control. In the late nineteenth century, Foucault explains in *The History of Sexuality,* "the analysis of heredity was placing sex (sexual relations, venereal diseases, matrimonial alliances, perversions) in a position of 'biological responsibility' with regard to the species: not only could sex be affected by its own diseases, it could also, if it was not controlled, transmit diseases or create others, that would afflict future generations."[3] Whereas in the Renaissance syphilis functioned as a religious symbol of the disease in the spirit, and during the Restoration became a political metaphor for the disease in the state, fin-de-siècle English culture treats it as a symbol of the disease in the family.[4]

In the 1890s too, research in medical science and cellular pathology proved what had long been suspected: general paralysis of the insane, a form of madness that affected up to 70 percent of male asylum patients, was actually the terminal form of syphilis. This understanding of general paralysis—otherwise known as GPI, syphilitic insanity, syphilis of the brain, dementia paralytica, or cerebral syphilis—was the perfect confirmation of late Victorian psychiatry's belief in heredity and visible vice. Among special predisposing causes of insanity, wrote Sir George Savage, "heredity stands first in importance.... The torch of civilization is handed from father to son, and as with idiosyncracies of mind, so the very body itself exhibits well-defined marks of its parentage."[5] Medical psychiatrists believed that based on the model of dementia paralytica, other forms of insanity could also be traced to indisputable organic cause, and that the physical basis of all mental disease would soon be firmly established.

Indeed, Dr. C. F. Marshall, who had been the house surgeon for the London Lock Hospital, attributed hereditary insanity in general to the effects of syphilis: "We often read of vague references to a 'hereditary predisposition to nervous disease,' a 'hereditary tendency to insanity,' etc. It would be far more rational to regard these 'hereditary tendencies' as nothing more or less than a predisposition to nervous and mental disease due to hereditary syphilis." Marshall ominously concluded, "Considering the predilection of syphilis for the nervous system, it is remarkable that insanity is not more widespread than it is."[6]

In its association with prostitution, adultery, perversity, and violence, furthermore, the characteristics of syphilitic insanity seemed to violate and subvert all of the society's most potent moral norms, to break all the bourgeois rules of sexual and social conduct. The popular image of the male paralytic was established by medical texts, quack advertisements, and sensational literature. "Extreme and sudden violence," according to Dr. Thomas J. Austin, author of the first English textbook on GPI, was the most usual cause of the paralytic's admission to the lunatic asylum, and in most cases the paralytic's wife was the injured victim. Within the asylum, most furious maniacal attacks came on at night, in which "noise, restlessness, dirty, destructive habits, and . . . raving, are all carried to an extreme pitch. I have seen no mania comparable with paralytic furor." Toward morning, Austin added, the frenzied patient became calm and slept; the next day he appeared "quite tranquil."[7]

Dr. Henry Maudsley, the intellectual leader of the Darwinian group in English psychiatry, also emphasized the personality changes that could more gradually transform a solid citizen into a criminal:

> A man who has been hitherto temperate in all his habits, prudent and industrious in business, and exemplary in the relations of life, undergoes a great change of character, gives way to dissipation of all sorts, launches into reckless speculations in business, and becomes indifferent

to his wife, his family, the obligations of his position; his surprised friends see only the effects of vice, and . . . after a time, they hear that he is in the police court accused of assault or stealing. . . . The dissipation, the speculation, and the theft itself were, as they often are, the first symptoms of general paralysis of the insane.[8]

Overall, then, syphilitic insanity was characterized by a virtually complete perversion of moral sense. The paralytic might begin with euphoria or with fits, but in any case, as Dr. W. Julius Mickle explained in his essay on the disease for the *Dictionary of Psychological Medicine,* his acts "cease to be guided, as formerly, by religion, altruism, sense of morality, or duty, patriotism, love of family, of truth, of friendship, of beauty."[9]

In a European context, this violently transgressive figure seemed to correspond to the privileged decadence of the *poète maudit.* In France, particularly, male writers had become obsessed with the idea of syphilis and madness as the symptoms and the stigmata of creative genius. The French physician Joseph Moreau had argued that genius itself was a hereditary abnormality, a pathological condition linked to neurosis; and such French writers as Baudelaire, the Goncourt brothers, Flaubert, Maupassant, and Daudet celebrated their syphilis, hallucinations, ennuis, depressions, seizures and tremors, in the confidence that their "horror of life," their embrace of *le mal,* their sense that health was "plebeian and contemptible" made them superior to the bourgeoisie and representative of a more advanced, if less hardy, creative humanity.[10] Unlike their French brothers, however, the English were always skeptical of this romantic rationalization of insanity and disease. In the spirit of British empiricism, Havelock Ellis conducted a statistical study of British genius, and concluded that it was not significantly correlated with madness.[11] Others expressed a detached and urbane view of French excesses. "The Frenchmen are passing away," Henry James wrote to Robert Louis Stevenson in 1893, "Maupassant dying of locomotor paralysis, the fruit of fabulous habits, I am told. *Je n'en sais rien,* but I shall miss him."[12] Although there were persistent rumors that various English writers, such as Stevenson himself, Wilde, Bram Stoker, and later James Joyce, were paying for their own fabulous habits with syphilitic infections, for the English, syphilitic insanity was never a beautiful *fleur du mal.*[13]

English attitudes must be understood in the historical and social contexts that were defined for women and for men. Victorian men and Victorian women grew up with different kinds of knowledge about syphilis, and consequently different ideas about its symbolic relationship to their own psyches. The hideous ravages of syphilis, from an enormous and Miltonic list of skin disorders—macules, papules, tubercules, pustules, blebs, tumors, lesions, scales, crusts, ulcers, chancres, gummas, fissures, and scars—to cardiovascular disturbances, locomotor ataxia, tabes, blindness, and dementia, made the disease a powful deterrent in the theological and moral reform campaigns to control male sexuality. The breakdown in some of the old sexual prohibitions, the tacit recognition by the 1890s that masturbation, for example, was nearly universal, may have escalated the terms of the debate; and many Victorian physicians, such as Dr. Samuel Solly, regarded syphilis "as a blessing . . . inflicted by the Almighty to act as a restraint upon the indulgence of evil passions."[14] In *The Pathology of Mind,* Maudsley argued that where there was the most sexual spontaneity, pleasure, and intensity of feeling, there was also the most danger of infection: "Illicit relations," he warned, "provoke more passionate indulgence, since custom stales and stolen pleasures are sweet; and I have known general paralytics, married as well as unmarried, whose secret illicit amours, quite unsuspected until disclosed by the calamity, were thus pathologically avenged."[15]

In the Victorian home, handbooks of popular medicine made images of the syphilitic wages of premarital and extramarital sin available for the instruction of the young boy. "Walter," the author of *My Secret Life,* recalled being terrified as a child by a book about venereal disease shown to him by his godfather:

"The illustrations in the book, of faces covered with scabs, blotches, and eruptions, took such hold of my mind that for twenty years afterwards the fear was not quite eradicated."[16] Boys and men were also made constantly aware of the dangers of venereal infection by newspaper advertisements for an exotic catalogue of patent antisyphilis medicines, injections, and ointments: Curtis's Manhood, Sir Samuel Hannay's Specific, Dr. Brodum's Botanical Syrup, Dr. Morse's Invigorating Cordial, Naples Soap, Armenian Pills, Bumstead's Gleet Cure, Red Drops, The Unfortunate's Friend, and Davy's Lac-Elephantis, a popular nostrum that claimed to be the medicated milk of elephants.[17] In Blackpool, a wax museum owned by Louis Tussaud displayed graphic models of syphilitic disfigurement to deter sailors "from patronizing the whores along the dock road."[18]

As a result of this publicity, and because anxieties about syphilis were so intense, Victorian nerve specialists complained of rampant syphilophobia among their male patients. Dr. William Acton explained that like hysteria, syphilophobia

> will assume every form of venereal disease found or described in books . . . every trifling ailment will be exaggerated until the medical man is unable to distinguish what his patient really feels and what he supposes he feels. Did isolated cases only now and then occur, perhaps they might not deserve attention, but so numerous are they in a large capital like London, so anxious are the sufferers to obtain relief by consulting every man who can be supposed to offer them any means of relief, that they spend fortunes in travelling about and visiting every quack.[19]

Although the prostitute had become the official scapegoat for the sexual anxieties of the male community, the male syphilophobic fantasy drew on the guilty acknowledgment of a monstrous sexual self. The disease was the eruption of a repressed desire, the surfacing of a secret life. As Basil Hallward warns Dorian Gray in Wilde's novel, "People talk of secret vices. There are no such things. If a wretched man has a vice, it shows itself in the lines of his mouth, the droop of his eyelids, and moulding of his hands even."[20]

Women's attitudes, however, were based on a different moral ideology. For respectable women, syphilis had nothing to do with marital transgression, secret vices, or monstrous desires; it was more likely the wages of ignorance than the wages of sin. In most cases, it occurred as the result of marital intercourse with promiscuous husbands, who communicated the disease to their wives with "almost unfailing regularity."[21] Although prostitutes constituted the largest category of female syphilitics and general paralytics, the plight of the diseased wife also generated a potent mythology. One popular manual of venereology gave instructions to the doctor on breaking the bad news to a syphilitic wife. Although Victorian boys were lectured and warned, bright girls, the girls likely to become New Women, learned about syphilis in reading forbidden medical books like the manual just mentioned or the frightening book "Walter"'s godfather displayed to him. Cecily Hamilton made the discovery very young: "By the idle opening of a book . . . I remember the thought which flashed into my mind—we are told we have got to be married, but we are never told *that*! It was my first revolt against the compulsory nature of the trade of marriage."[22] For these feminists, syphilitic insanity was the product of man's viciousness and represented innocent woman's entrapment and victimization. The prolonged feminist campaign against the Contagious Diseases Acts educated women to understand that prostitutes were hapless victims of male lust and that the laws gave sanction to "a vast male conspiracy to degrade women."[23] Perverted men, feminists argued, spread syphilis through homosexual acts and then infected the prostitute. "Among men," Josephine Butler wrote in a private communication, "the disease is almost universal at one time or another."[24] The imagined male conspiracy of doctors, legislators, and libertines coalesced in the rumor that Jack the Ripper was a mad doctor avenging himself on prostitutes for a case of syphilis.[25]

Most important, feminists viewed syphilis as scientific evidence that the sins of the fathers were visited upon the children.

It was well known that the worst physical as well as mental effects of syphilis were hereditary. Congenital syphilis, which the Victorians called "syphilis of the innocents," is even more devastating than the acquired form of the disease, because it has already entered the secondary phase and begun to attack the nervous system. During the nineteenth century, the infant mortality rate for children of syphilitics was exceptionally high; from 60 percent to 90 percent died in their first year. Often deformed or retarded, the syphilitic infant was a pitiful sight, described by one doctor as a "small, wizened, atrophied, weakly, sickly creature," resembling a "monkey or a little old man."[26] Suffering, apish, shriveled, and prematurely aged, these syphilitic children appeared to feminists as living symbols of the devolutionary force of male vice.

Women's fantasies about syphilis thus centered on the fear of marital penetration and contamination, and on anxieties about hereditary transmission of the disease to children. The seminal fluid might be a deadly injection, and some extreme feminists, like Frances Swiney, believed that sperm itself was a virulent poison and that conjugal intercourse should be restricted to annual occasions.[27]

It is easy to ridicule such fantasies, or to see them as neurotic causes of the sexual anaesthesia that Havelock Ellis found characteristic of late-nineteenth-century women, yet late Victorian medicine itself had endorsed both the view of the disease and the ideology of the hereditary taint. Furthermore, there are enough cases of women writers, from Violet Hunt (the mistress of Ford Madox Ford) to Isak Dinesen, whose lives were wrecked by syphilitic infection, to make us take their anxieties seriously.[28]

Freud's case study of the hysterical girl he called Dora shows how completely even the most advanced psychiatrists of the fin de siècle accepted the theory of biological responsibility and the sins of the fathers. Dora had been brought for analysis by her father, whom Freud had treated for syphilis before his marriage. In the course of describing a dream, she revealed, to Freud's astonishment, that she knew what her father's illness had been, and that "she assumed that he had handed on his bad health to her by heredity." Freud, too, believed this to be the case. Noting that "a *strikingly high* percentage" of the hysterical women he had treated psychoanalytically had fathers suffering from "tabes or general paralysis," Freud had concluded that "syphilis in the male parent is a very relevant factor in the aetiology of the neuropathic constitution of children." Yet when Dora made her statement, Freud "was careful not to tell her" that he agreed.[29] In this specific instance, as well as in his general indifference to Dora's social situation, Freud both protected Dora's father and deprived her of vital reassurance that her "fantasies" of paternal infection might be legitimate.

Dora's famous second dream, in which on the day of her father's funeral she "went calmly to her room and began reading a big book that lay on her writing-table," takes on renewed significance in the contexts of late Victorian medical beliefs. When the contaminating and discrediting father is dead, Dora, like Olive Schreiner and Cecily Hamilton, can read calmly about sexuality and venereal disease in the big book that Freud interpreted as a medical encyclopedia. The sexual anxieties associated with syphilis are thus connected to intellectual and imaginative constraint. "If her father was dead," Freud observes, "she could read or love as she pleased."[30] To this we might add, noting where the book lay, that she could also *write* as she pleased. Dora's dream suggests that the syphilitic father was an image of creative as well as sexual censorship for women of the fin de siècle, an obstacle in the path of erotic and literary freedom.

In fact, fin-de-siècle feminist writers applied the new terminology of Darwinian science to the study of male sexuality and discovered biological sins that could lead to general retrogression. "Man in any age or country is liable to revert to a state of savagery," wrote Mona Caird in a series on marriage in the *Westminster Review*.[31] Taking to heart Darwinian arguments about women's self-sacrifice for the good of the species, and sustained by the Victorian belief in women's passionlessness, English radical feminists envisioned themselves as chaste yet maternal heralds of a higher race. In their stories, sexuality is purged, projected, or transcended; sexual disease is male and has nothing to do with the female self.

Rather than protest against evolutionary theories of femininity, moreover, feminists appropriated them. In what seems like a defiant response to the jeremiads of Darwinian psychiatrists against unsexed intellectual women, women who were withering and drying up, "Ellis Ethelmer" celebrated the gradual disappearance of the "menstrual habit" among the Newest Women of the age: "Let it be remembered that menstruation is not an indispensable requisite of either health or maternity," Ethelmer wrote in 1895; "with the healthier living and physical training of women in the present day, there is no doubt that the obnoxious phenomenon is already distinctly diminishing in force and prevalence."[32]

And some feminists fantasized the ultimate biological transcendence and the ultimate evolutionary goal of virgin birth. "If one could only have a child . . . without a husband or the disgrace," yearns a woman in George Egerton's *Keynotes* (1894); "Ugh, the disgusting men."[33] In the many feminist utopias written by English and American women of the fin de siècle, we can see numerous expressions of the wish for motherhood without the need for dangerous exposure to intercourse and/or disease. Works like Charlotte Perkins Gilman's *Herland* (1915) depict women evolved beyond mere physical reproduction. These inhabitants of a female society bear daughters through parthenogenesis; sexuality has been so thoroughly eliminated that *Herland* is also free of lesbianism. Their Amazon society has no men, no sexual desire, no syphilis, and no insanity.

In the protest fiction of Sarah Grand, Olive Schreiner, Elizabeth Robins and Ménie Dowie, themes that had been covertly and marginally broached by Victorian women novelists (such as George Eliot in *The Mill on the Floss*, where Wakem's illegitimate son, Jetsome, or his crippled legitimate son, Philip, may be paying for the sins of the father), were given full narrative attention. Sarah Grand's bestseller *The Heavenly Twins* (1893) pioneered the feminist attack on the syphilitic father, offering two heroines who make the right and the wrong choices about marrying syphilitic men. Edith marries a syphilitic naval officer, blind to the clues that he has a venereal disease, although he has "small, peery" eyes, has deserted the mother of his sickly illegitimate son, and has a head that "shelved backwards like an ape's." Edith hopes to reform him by her love, but within a year she is tottering under the "shadow of an awful form of insanity," and her syphilitic infant son is "old, old already, and exhausted with suffering." Edith quickly sinks into dementia, shrieking "I want to kill—I want to kill *him*. I want to kill that monstrous child!" The horrified women watching around her bed listen to her raving against "the arrangement of society which has made it possible for me and my child to be sacrificed in this way," and Grand warns the reader that "the same thing may happen now to any mother—to any daughter—and will happen so long as we refuse to know and resist."[34]

For male writers of the fin de siècle, however, the literary uses and meaning of syphilitic insanity were very different. In late Victorian male fantasy fiction, feminist ideology comes under attack, and syphilophobic anxieties appear in the form of fear of female sexuality and intensified misogyny. Bram Stoker's *Dracula* (1897), for example, is often described by feminist critics as a thinly veiled fantasy of contaminating female sexuality, a novel whose central anxiety is "the fear of the devouring woman."[35] This rapacious figure is also connected to the New Woman and her insistence on sexual information; as Stoker's Mina observes, "Some of the 'New Women' writers will someday start an idea that men and women should be allowed to see each other asleep before proposing or accepting." Women seem empowered in the novel. Dracula himself is outnumbered by the sisterhood of seductive female vampires who are part of his incestuous harem and who arouse feelings both of thrilling sensuality and of horrified disgust in the men they offer to kiss. Dracula's daughters are sexually aggressive while men are chaste and passive. Ecstatically waiting to be attacked by one vampire, Jonathan Harker observes that she "licked her lips like an animal, till I could see in the moonlight the moisture shining on the scarlet lips and on the red tongue as it lapped the white sharp teeth." The sexual act is represented as contact with a wet red mouth filled with sharp teeth, a *vagina dentata* that is also infected and unclean. The physical and moral transformations suffered by the innocent victims of Dracula in the novel suggest the dangers of syphilis, but here women undergo the worst effects, and the men must "save" them by such violent medical interventions as decapitation and phallic stakes through the heart.[36]

Lucy Westenra, the first of Dracula's victims, is temporarily protected from his embrace by wreaths of garlic draped around her by Dr. Van Helsing. In her white nightdress, as she herself notes in her diary, she is "like Ophelia in the play, with 'virgin crants and maiden strewments'"—but a sinister fin-de-siècle Ophelia, who will later rise from the grave in a white shroud to become the vampire who kills children on Hampstead Heath: "Lucy Westenra, but yet how changed. The sweetness was turned to adamantine, heartless cruelty, and the purity to voluptuous wantonness."[37] While Dracula, with his peculiar physiognomy and unnatural habits, resembles the syphilitic men who prey on the heroines of feminist novels, the mad and infected Lucy, like Sarah Grand's Edith, turns her aggression first against children.

Lucy's dual nature, her susceptibility to mesmeric trance, and her somnambulistic habits mark her as a nervous heroine of the fin de siècle, a sister to Dora and other female hysterics.[38] But Stoker's dark fantasy seems most closely connected with Zola's horrifying description of the syphilitic death of the prostitute Nana, a potent counterpart to feminist allegories of the diseased male. At the end of Zola's novel, the dying Nana is abandoned by her lover; regarding her corpse, her maids are struck by a horror as great as that of Stoker's heroes before Lucy the vampire: "She's changed, she's changed!"[39]

Zola's deathbed description of Nana, in a novel widely read by the Victorian male avant-garde, must have made an indelible impression:

> She was the fruit of the charnel house . . . a shovelful of corrupted flesh thrown down on the pillow. The pustules had invaded the whole of the face . . . and on that formless pulp, where the features had ceased to be traceable, they already resembled some decaying damp from the grave. One eye . . . had completely foundered among bubbling purulence, and the other, which remained half open, looked like a deep, black, ruinous hole. The nose was still suppurating. Quite a reddish crust was peeling from one of the cheeks and invading the mouth, which it distorted into a horrible grin. And over this loathsome and grotesque mask of death the hair, the beautiful hair, still blazed like sunlight and flowed downward in rippling gold. Venus was rotting.[40]

Like the suppurating Nana, Lucy becomes a "foul thing," emblem of a certain kind of fin-de-siècle feminine ending immortalized by the male imagination. H. Rider Haggard's queenly Ayesha, the sex goddess of *She,* also has her final metamorphosis in dissolution; her beautiful hair falls out as she shrivels into an apelike monster.

Yet some male writers were able to make the first break from the moral strangleholds of Victorian sexual anxiety. In the work of Ibsen, Wilde, Stevenson, Hardy, Wells, and Joyce, syphilophobia is not invariably represented as female monstrosity or a rotting Venus; and the sins of the fathers are not lust and vice, but ignorance, guilt, shame, and fear. For this literary avant-garde, syphilis provides the iconography for stories of the mask, the double, and the shadow, and for studies of divided selves in a society where repression and hypocrisy are forms of sexual disease.

In Stevenson's *Dr. Jekyll and Mr. Hyde* (1886), Jekyll is an anti-Darwinian scientist who rejects the positivist beliefs of his generation, and who has been experimenting with ways to release the psyche from its bondage to physical existence. A social as well as intellectual renegade, Jekyll's needs to pursue pleasure and yet to live up to the exacting moral standards of his bleak professional community have committed him to "a profound duplicity of life," accompanied by "an almost morbid sense of shame." Coming to acknowledge his sexual longings and fantasies, Jekyll longs to separate his mind and his body, his intellect and his desire: "If each, I told myself, could be housed in separable identities, life would be relieved of all that was unbearable."⁴¹

The "hairy and libidinous" Hyde, embodiment of Jekyll's irregularities and secret appetites, is described in the physical vocabulary of syphilitic deformity and regression; he is "abnormal," "troglodytic," "ape-like" and "dwarfish," and he generates "disgust, loathing, and fear" in the men who see him. Jekyll's metamorphosis into Hyde, first drug-induced and then involuntary, suggests the dramatic personality changes of syphilitic dementia catalogued by Darwinian psychiatrists. Hyde's "complete moral insensibility" and his impulsive violent crimes resemble the "paralytic furor" described by doctors like Thomas Austin. As Hyde's crimes become known, Jekyll's friends speculate that the doctor is being blackmailed, paying for youthful transgression: "the ghost of some old sin, the cancer of some concealed disgrace." Even Jekyll's frenzied search for the antidote recalls the syphilophobe's pursuit of remedies like the Unfortunate's Friend. Jekyll's suicide can be seen as the last act of degeneration and dementia, or as a desperate escape from public disgrace and paralytic decline. The liberation of Jekyll's mad desire shakes "the very fortress of identity." Stevenson represents the split not only in the Jekyll-Hyde personalities but also in the doctor's residence, the "fortress" in which the dual identities are "housed." In the front, there is prosperity, "a great air of wealth and comfort," and a luxurious vestibule warmed by "a bright, open fire." In the rear is the secret windowless laboratory, filled with disgusting "chemical apparatus," and bearing "in every feature the marks of prolonged and sordid negligence."[42] In discovering a way to separate the upper and nether aspects of his psyche, Jekyll destroys himself, even though the discovery is the pinnacle of his creative and scientific achievement. Divorced from its passionate drives, reason becomes an empty fortress; neglected and released from the union with the intellect, desire becomes syphilitic frenzy.

In Stevenson's fantasy of the diseased and divided self, passion seems to have no female source or object; the meditation on evil is all in terms of the masculine psyche. The story's narrators—the lawyer Utterson, the physician Lanyon, and finally Jekyll himself—are all bachelors, even celibates. Whereas the typical Victorian male reformer (like Gladstone) sublimated his own sexual fantasies by rescuing fallen women, Utterson boasts that he is frequently "the last good influence in the lives of down-going men." The reader assumes that in Jekyll's life, "nine-tenths a life of effort, virtue, and control," Hyde's irregularities are sexual.[43] But there were no women in the story until the 1920 film version with John Barrymore misrepresented Stevenson's plot by adding a good and a bad woman to correspond to the conflicting demands of society and the self, an emendation that all subsequent film versions have included.

Actually Jekyll seems to be Hyde's parthenogenic father, with "more than a father's interest," as Hyde has "more than a son's indifference." Feeling Hyde writhing in his flesh, "struggling to be born," Jekyll feels the full horror of his sexual sins.[44] And Hyde, in his murder of the elderly Sir Danvers Carew, and his destruction of the letters and portrait of Jekyll's father, seems to be attempting symbolic acts of parricide that release him from patriarchal heredity.

There are no women in Dorian Gray's downfall either (except for the fatuous Sibyl Vane); Dorian is poisoned by his three aesthetic fathers: Basil Hallward, who appropriates his image for art; Lord Henry Wootton, who encourages him to yield to the desire for the things the world's "monstrous laws have made monstrous and unlawful," (26) and the French decadent J. K. Huysmans, whose novel *A Rebours* introduces him to the worship of the senses.[45]

Like Stevenson, Oscar Wilde uses the physical imagery of syphilis to embody the madness that possesses Dorian Gray. Dorian's vice is like "a horrible malady" (208); the changes that take place in the portrait as the "leprosies of sin" (175) eat it away are like the progressive pathologies of syphilis: "hideous face" (173), "warped lips," "coarse bloated hands" (143), a red stain that has "crept like a horrible disease over the wrinkled fingers" (246), "misshapen body and failing limbs" (143), a general air of the bestial, sodden and unclean. "Was it to become a monstrous and loathsome thing," Dorian wonders, "to be hidden away in a locked room?" (119). The sudden and uncontrollable frenzy in which "the mad passions of a hunted animal" (176) seize Dorian and he murders Basil Hallward, even his abrupt rejection of Sibyl Vane, suggest the psychology of general paralysis. In this novel, too, suicide is the final stage of the dementia created by giving way to the tyranny of the passions.

Dorian flirts with Darwinism, playing with ideas of biological determinism, and finding solace in the notion that "the passion for sin" is programmed into the cells of the brain, so that sexual impulses are irresistible. Yet Wilde is also contemptuous of the materialist and "shallow psychology" (159) of the Darwinians. Like Stevenson, he insists on the complexity of the psyche, its capacity to house myriad identities and desires. Dorian's "sin" destroys him because the "harsh uncomely puritanism" (146) of the day, a puritanism supported by women and by the marriage system, has never allowed the inherited multiform lives of male passion to evolve along with those of thought; "the senses . . . had remained savage and animal merely because the world had sought to starve them into submission . . . instead of aiming at making them elements of a new spirituality, of which a fine instinct for beauty was to be the dominant characteristic" (145).

In a more tolerant society, one in which male desire was not confined by female social convention, Wilde hints, sexual desire would evolve away from perversity, violence, and disease, into something like aesthetic appreciation.

H. G. Wells's *The Time Machine* (1895) transposes the separation of body and mind from an aesthetic to a scientific context. Wells imagines the "savage and animal" senses as they might become in the remote future if they continued to evolve separately from the rest of the psyche, which in its innocent "spirituality" would follow its own evolutionary path. The simian Morlocks, "bleached, obscene and nocturnal" creatures of the nether world of appetite and rapine, inhabit a dark underground labyrinth like Jekyll's laboratory or Dorian's foul dens. When the Time Traveller descends, it is as if he has penetrated the mysteries of the body itself. He is surrounded by the "throb and hum" of machinery, the "heavy smell" of blood, and especially by the nauseating sense of physical contact, the "soft palps" and "filthily cold" invading hands that feel all over his skin. The loathsome Morlocks, so suggestive of syphilitic deformity and its hereditary results, are the final stages of sexual degeneration, male sewer-dwellers who embody both upper-class fears of the working class, and the feminist dread of masculine desire. In one sense, the Eloi, tiny and exquisitely helpless inhabitants of the Upper-World, are a parody of Dorian Gray's decadent aesthetics. But they also represent the evolutionary result of the feminist avant-garde, refined and spiritualized into an infantile nervous perfection that can no longer think or create. In Eloi society, the Time Traveller notes, there is no syphilis: "the ideal preventive medicine was attained . . . I saw no evidence of any contagious diseases during all my stay."[46] Yet without the Darwinian grindstone of pain, desire, and repression, humanity grows dull and languid, and decays. That the Morlocks feed upon the Eloi is Wells's mordant response to the sexless feminist utopias.

For Stevenson, Wilde, and Wells, sexual disease and syphilitic insanity were the excrescencies of an unhealthy society, one that systematically suppressed desire and that also produced anxious fathers, febrile art, and divided and disfigured sons. In Ibsen's *Ghosts,* the most famous of all nineteenth-century works about sexual disease, the theme of syphilitic insanity was significantly turned back on women, and on social morality. Ibsen's young artist-hero Oswald Alving goes mad in the final stages of cerebral syphilis inherited from his promiscuous father. But Oswald's mother is forced to recognize that her own pious conventionality and frigidity, rather than male viciousness, had driven her husband to prostitutes. The sins in the plays are not those of the father. As Ibsen's still shocking conclusion forces us to see, the devoted mother is the real executioner of the son, and the real enemy of his artistic genius. Ibsen's ghosts are thus not the invisible spirochetes of syphilis, but the internalized and virulent prohibitions of religion and bourgeois morality. These, Mrs. Alving declares, constitute the true hereditary taint: "It is not only what we have inherited from our fathers and mothers that exists again in us, but all sorts of old dead ideas and all kinds of old dead beliefs . . . They are dormant, and we can never be rid of them. Whenever I take up a newspaper and read it, I fancy I see ghosts creeping between the lines. There must be ghosts all over the world. . . . And we are so miserably afraid of the light."[47]

Produced in London in March 1891, the play provoked an outburst of horror, outrage, and disgust unprecedented in the history of English criticism: "an open drain; a loathsome sore unbandaged; a dirty act done publicly." The hysteria over *Ghosts*—over five hundred articles about it were published in England during the following year—suggests how threatened conventional readers felt by Ibsen's intimations that the principles of conjugal obligation, feminine purity, and religious inhibition were not the forces of spiritual evolution but of aesthetic and sexual degeneration.[48]

If *Ghosts* is the *locus classicus* of syphilitic insanity, Hardy's

Jude the Obscure (1895) is indeed the consummate literary text
of late Victorian psychiatry, incorporating the degenerate characters of the ambitious and intemperate working man, the
neurasthenic and sexually anxious New Woman, and the morbid
and blighted child. Although syphilis does not figure centrally
in the text, but hovers on its Gothic margins, Hardy's novel follows Ibsen in turning the question of sexual disease back on the
woman.

In his postscript to the novel, Hardy described Sue as "the
woman of the feminist movement—the intellectualized, emancipated bundle of nerves that modern conditions were produc-
ing, mainly in cities as yet, who does not recognize the necessity
for most of her sex to follow marriage as a profession."[49] In
her aversion to sex and her view of marriage as a "sordid contract" (323), Sue resembles the celibate heroines of Gilman
or Grand, and to some utopian feminists of the period, Sue
was indeed an exemplary heroine. Jane Hume Clapperton
praised her as one whose sexuality evolved from "the lower
reaches of pure sensation" to "a higher kind of tender sentiment . . . energized from the intellectual plane," in which "all
the grossness, i.e. the coarser vibrations of primitive love, are
transmuted into the finer vibrations of sympathetic, altruistic
feeling."[50] Furthermore, as Hardy explained in a letter to Edmund Gosse, "though she has children, her intimacies with Jude
have never been more than occasional . . . they occupy separate
rooms."[51] Sue's births are nearly virgin ones. But she is also
frigid and neurotic, atrophied and vulnerable. When she breaks
down in grief over the death of her children, she forces herself
into a "fanatic prostitution" (437) with Phillotson, a sexual
immolation that Hardy presents as the masochistic mirror-
opposite of her fear of the body and of the male.

Jude too is doomed by the inexorable laws of nature and
inheritance. Late Victorian psychiatrists had warned that work-
ing-class men who tried to better themselves were risking madness from a kind of intellectual work their heredity had not

prepared them to handle. Sir George Savage had seen "constant examples in Bethlem of young men, who, having left the plough for the desk, have found, after years of struggle, that their path was barred by social or other hindrances, and disappointment, worry, and the solitude of a great city have produced insanity of an incurable type."[52] Jude is chiefly broken, however, by his sexuality. Here Hardy was deeply ambivalent. The transgressive sexual images of Stevenson and Wilde, of carnivalesque debauchery and misrule, make a dim appearance in Hardy's realistic narrative with Arabella's pigsty, with the brawling itinerant carnival troupe that appears to defend Phillotson's morals, and with the Great Wessex Agricultural Fair. But for Hardy, fairs, like the ones in *The Mayor of Casterbridge* where Henchard sells his wife, were shameful occasions. And if male sexuality leads to drunkenness, fighting, disease, and transgression, female sexuality, as in *Dracula,* threatens the male with castration. Jude thinks he wants Sue to desire him, but at heart he prefers her "phantasmal, bodiless" (324) sexlessness to the full-bodied hoggish sensuality of Arabella. As in *The Woodlanders* and other Hardy novels, marriage is a biological trap, a man-trap baited by female allure. Jude wonders whether "the women are to blame . . . or is it the artificial system of things under which the normal sex-impulses are turned into devilish domestic gins and springes" (279). When, on their wedding night, Arabella casually removes her false hair, Jude realizes how thoroughly *he* has been undone by the domestic gin that is also a *vagina dentata,* a hairy springe. Like Nana, Ayesha, or Lucy, she too is horribly changed, reverting to the beast. The misogynistic tableau of the lady's dressing room goes back to Swift; but Hardy gives it the frisson of fin-de-siècle morbidity.

The most troubling character in the novel has always been Little Father Time, the offspring of Jude's botched marriage to the porcine Arabella. His entrance into the novel shatters its structure of narrative realism, and many critics have complained that he seems to come from another planet or another book.

Little Father Time's murder of his half-brothers and sisters, and his suicide, Havelock Ellis protested, removed the story from "the large field of common life into the small field of the police court or the lunatic asylum," and turned it into a case history of "gross pathological degenerescence."[53]

Little Father Time, in my view, can best be understood in the contexts of the feminist protest fiction of the period, and of its conventions relating to the prematurely aged and psychologically disturbed syphilitic child. Hardy adapts these conventions to make Father Time a victim of spoiled heredity like his parents before, a "preternaturally old boy" (347) who pays with his sanity and his life for the intolerance, cruelty, and narrowness of his society. He is the mad child whose breakdown is the signifier of the conflicts, lies, and hypocrisies of the sexual system. He becomes, as Hardy says, "the whole tale of their situation. On that little shape had converged all the inauspiciousness and shadow which had darkened the first union of Jude, and all the accidents, mistakes, fears, errors, of the last. He was their nodal point, their focus, their expression in a single term. For the rashness of those parents he had groaned, for their ill-assortment he had quaked, and for the misfortunes of these he had died" (411).

Like *Ghosts*, *Jude the Obscure* was greeted with outrage, accused of obscenity, Ibsenity, decadence and degeneration, and ritually compared to slime and filth. Although Wells, Swinburne, and later, Lawrence, admired the novel, many of Hardy's female literary contemporaries saw it as a contemptible study of sexual pathology.[54] During this period of conflict between male and female writers over the representation of sexuality, there also begin to be insistent pronouncements by men on the essential relationship of male sexuality and imaginative power, declaring that, as Gerard Manley Hopkins had stated in 1886, "the begetting of one's thoughts on paper" is "a kind of male gift."[55]

Furthermore, these claims to a phallic literary monopoly came at the end of the richest and most influential period of female literary creativity in English history, and they signal a masculine reappropriation of the field. After the death of George Eliot in 1880, male professional jealousies and animosities that had perhaps been suppressed erupted in critical abuse of women's emasculating effect on the English novel. In 1883 Havelock Ellis could praise Hardy by comparing him to George Eliot, for, as Ellis observed, "it seems now to stand beyond question that the most serious work in modern English fiction . . . has been done by women."[56] Ten years later, after essays like George Moore's "Literature at Nurse" and Hardy's "Candour in English Fiction," such comparisons were odious. Women novelists were viewed as shriveled prudes whose malign influence enervated a virile male genre. In the 1890s, after a century in which women writers had shaped the traditions of English fiction, male writers at last achieved unquestioned dominance of the novel.[57]

H. Rider Haggard's immensely popular "adventure" novel, *She* (1887), provides a fascinating demonstration of the battle for paternal supremacy that seems to be waged beneath the surface of much fin-de-siècle male fantasy fiction. *She* tells the story of the journey to the Dark Continent of Africa by two Cambridge University scholars to find the legendary city of Kôr, ruled by an immortal white goddess. On one Freudian level, the men are penetrating the mysterious darkness of female sexuality, finding in its deepest vaginal cavern the beautiful and seductive queen Ayesha. Yet other details suggest a more historically specific reading. Cambridge is presented as the last stronghold of pure, homosocial, and potentially homosexual, masculinity, during the decade in which women were pressing for admission to the colleges and to university degrees. The older of the men is a bachelor don who has adopted and jealously raised the younger, hiring a manservant rather than a female nurse, because he is "determined to have no woman to lord it over me about the child and steal his affections from me." Confronted by the matriarchal society of Ayesha's tribe, the Amahagger,

the Cambridge scholars are appalled by women's sexual assertive-
ness in a kinship system where "descent is traced only through
the line of the mother, and . . . they never pay attention to, or
even acknowledge any man as their father, even when their male
parentage is perfectly well-known." The power of Ayesha is
explicitly compared to that of Queen Victoria, and implicitly
suggests the literary reign of George Eliot, a troubling female
precursor for Haggard and his male contemporaries. Ayesha's
destruction reflects not only Haggard's extreme revulsion from
female sexuality, and his wish to appropriate the maternal function, but also his fear of an autonomous and self-defining female literary tradition.[58] Women writers at the turn of the
century, however, were confined by a conservative sexual
ideology that was an aesthetic dead end. While male writers ex-
plored the multiplicity of the self, the myriad fluid lives of
men, women were limited by the revived biological essentialism
of post-Darwinian thought. The unchanging nature of woman
as pure spirit made good politics but bad fiction. Feminist psychology was too monolithic to provide a mothering-forth in
literature, and its celibacy was increasingly sterile. The last
stand of fin-de-siècle feminism against the sins of the fathers
was Christabel Pankhurst's *The Great Scourge and How to End
It* (1913). Declaring that 75 percent to 80 percent of English
men were infected with venereal disease, Pankhurst called for an
end to the double standard. Her solution, however, was *not* female sexual liberation—"Votes for women and Wild Oats for
women!"—but male abstinence: "Votes for women and chastity
for men!" Until men became as virtuous as women, Pankhurst
concluded, and as deeply concerned about "fatherhood, father-
craft, and the duties . . . of paternity," marriage was too dangerous to attempt.[59] Not for another decade could feminist writers
acknowledge that sexual dis-ease could be a creative paralysis
and that the great scourge had taken place not only in men's
bodies but also in women's minds.

The literary mythologies of syphilis died out on the eve of

the Great War. Syphilis lost its mystery in medicine by 1913 with the discovery of the spirochete, Salvarsan, and the Wassermann blood test. In literature, male writers had redefined the locus of vice, had changed the subject of the debate from the sins of the fathers to the sexuality of sons and lovers and the neurotic frigidity of mothers and wives. That women writers, in the process, had dropped out of the Great Tradition, or to put it more accurately, had been pushed out of it, was one of the side effects of the modernist transformation.

Finally, World War I was a Great Scourge that could not be contained by individual moral sanction, a mad enterprise on a scale that made Wells's apocalyptic predictions or Pankhurst's fulminations seem puny. It was in one of Siegfried Sassoon's angry poems from the trenches that (he later boasted) the word "syphilitic" was first brought into the sacred and pristine realm of English verse.[60] And by that time, as the generation of 1914 knew, the sins of the fathers to which they were all being sacrificed were not the sins of desire but of blood.

NOTES

1. Susan Sontag, *Illness as Metaphor* (New York: Vintage Books, 1979), pp. 58–59.

2. See Judith Walkowitz, *Prostitution and Victorian Society* (Cambridge: Cambridge University Press, 1982), pp. 48–53.

3. Michel Foucault, *The History of Sexuality,* trans. Robert Hurley, vol. 1 (New York: Vintage Books, 1980), p. 118.

4. I am indebted to Annabel Patterson for this observation.

5. George Savage, *Insanity and Allied Neuroses* (Philadelphia: Henry C. Lea, 1884), p. 37, quoted in Jane Marcus, "Virginia Woolf and Her Violin: Mothering, Madness, and Music," in *Virginia Woolf: Centennial Essays,* ed. Elaine Ginsburg and Laura Moss Gottlieb (Troy, N.Y.: Whitston, 1983). I am indebted to Marcus for an advance copy of this essay.

6. C. F. Marshall, *Syphilology and Venereal Disease* (New York: Wood, 1906), p. 216. For general histories of syphilology, see R. S. Morton,

Venereal Diseases (Harmondsworth: Penguin Books, 1974); Theodor Rosebury, *Microbes and Morals* (New York: Viking Press, 1971); and William J. Brown et al., *Syphilis and Other Venereal Diseases* (Cambridge, Mass.: Harvard University Press, 1970).

7. Thomas J. Austin, *A Practical Account of General Paralysis* (1859; repr., New York: Arno, 1976), pp. 23, 24.

8. Henry Maudsley, *Responsibility in Mental Disease* (London: Henry J. King & Co., 1874), pp. 74-75.

9. W. Julius Mickle, "General Paralysis of the Insane," *Dictionary of Psychological Medicine,* ed. D. Hack Tuke (Philadelphia: P. Blackiston, Son, & Co., 1892), 1:521.

10. See Roger Williams, *The Horror of Life* (Chicago: University of Chicago Press, 1980).

11. Havelock Ellis, *A Study in British Genius* (1904), cited in George Pickering, *Creative Malady* (London: George Allen & Unwin, 1974), p. 295.

12. Henry James to R. L. Stevenson, 1893, quoted in Leon Edel, *Henry James: The Middle Years: 1882-1895,* vol. 3 of *The Life of Henry James* (New York: J. B. Lippincott Co., 1962; repr., Avon Books, 1978), p. 177.

13. See, for example, H. Montgomery Hyde, *Oscar Wilde* (New York: Farrar, Straus & Giroux, 1975), pp. 181, 184; Phyllis Grosskurth, *Havelock Ellis* (New York: Alfred A. Knopf, 1980), p. 335.

14. Dr. Samuel Solly, *Medical Times and Gazette,* Feb. 25, 1860, p. 201, quoted in E. M. Sigsworth and T. J. Wyke, "A Study of Victorian Prostitution and Venereal Disease," in *Suffer and Be Still,* ed. Martha Vicinus (Bloomington: Indiana University Press, 1972), p. 72.

15. Henry Maudsley, *The Pathology of Mind* (London: Macmillan & Co., 1895), pp. 467-68. See also George Savage, "GPI," in T. C. Allbutt and H. D. Rolleston, *A System of Medicine* 2d ed. (London: Macmillan & Co., 1910), 8:349.

16. "Walter," *My Secret Life,* quoted in Brian Harrison, "Underneath the Victorians," *Victorian Studies* 10 (1967): 256. See also Lyndall Gordon, *Eliot's Early Years* (London: Oxford University Press, 1977), p. 27.

17. See Samuel Hynes, *The Edwardian Turn of Mind* (Princeton, N.J.: Princeton University Press, 1968), p. 256; John S. Haller and Robin M. Haller, *The Physician and Sexuality in Urban America* (Urbana: University of Illinois Press, 1974), pp. 264-65; *Davy's Lac-Elephantis* (London: J. Callow, 1815).

18. George Melly, "Let the Thoughtless Man Here Pause," *New Statesman,* Mar. 1, 1963, pp. 317-18.

19. William Acton, *A Practical Treatise on Diseases of the Urinary and*

Generative Organs (in Both Sexes) (London: John Churchill, 1851), pp. 602-3.

20. Oscar Wilde, *The Picture of Dorian Gray* (Harmondsworth: Penguin Books, 1977), pp. 166-67. All subsequent references to this novel are to this edition and are cited parenthetically by page numbers in the text.

21. James N. Hyde and Frank H. Montgomery, *Manual of Syphilis and the Venereal Diseases* (Philadelphia, 1895), p. 30.

22. Cecily Hamilton, *Marriage as a Trade* (New York: Moffat, Yard & Co., 1909), p. 73.

23. Walkowitz, *Prostitution and Victorian Society*, p. 128.

24. Josephine Butler, quoted in ibid, p. 130.

25. Judith Walkowitz, "Jack the Ripper and the Myth of Male Violence," *Feminist Studies* 8 (1982): 556.

26. Marshall, *Syphilology and Venereal Disease*, p. 306.

27. See Hynes, *Edwardian Turn of Mind*, p. 204.

28. See Arthur Mizener, *The Saddest Story: A Biography of Ford Madox Ford* (New York: World Publishing Co., 1971), p. 149; and Judith Thurman, *Isak Dinesen* (New York: St. Martin's Press, 1982), pp. 256-58.

29. Sigmund Freud, *Dora: An Analysis of a Case of Hysteria* (New York: Collier Books, 1964), pp. 93, 35-36, 93.

30. Freud, *Dora,* pp. 120, 121.

31. Mona Caird, "Phases of Human Development," *Westminster Review* 141 (1894): 38.

32. Ellis Ethelmer, *The Human Flower: A Simple Statement of the Physiology of Birth and the Relations of the Sexes* (London, 1895), p. 32. "Ellis Ethelmer" was the pen name of the feminist activist Elizabeth Wollstoneholme Elmy and her common-law husband, Ben Elmy. Letters in the Macmillan Collection at the British Library suggest that he did most of the writing.

33. George Egerton, "The Spell of the White Elf," *Keynotes* (London: Virago Press, 1983), p. 80.

34. Sarah Grand, *The Heavenly Twins* (London: Heinemann, 1894), pp. 178, 280. For a more extensive discussion of this literature, see Elaine Showalter, *A Literature of Their Own: British Women Novelists from Brontë to Lessing* (Princeton, N.J.: Princeton University Press), pp. 182-215.

35. Phyllis Roth, "Suddenly Sexual Women in Bram Stoker's *Dracula*," *Literature and Psychology* 27 (1977): 119.

36. Bram Stoker, *Dracula* (1897; repr., New York: Doubleday, Page & Co., 1921), pp. 91, 39. The sociohistorical contexts of Stoker's novel as a commentary on venereal disease are discussed by Carol A. Senf, "Dracula: Stoker's Response to the New Woman," *Victorian Studies* 26 (1982): 34-49.

37. Stoker, *Dracula,* pp. 211, 134.

38. See Nina Auerbach's fascinating discussion of Lucy in *Woman and the Demon* (Cambridge, Mass.: Harvard University Press, 1982), pp. 22–24.

39. Emile Zola, *Nana* (New York: Greystone Press, n.d.), p. 311.

40. Ibid.

41. Robert Louis Stevenson, *The Strange Case of Dr. Jekyll and Mr. Hyde and Other Stories* (Harmondsworth; Penguin Books, 1979), pp. 81, 82.

42. Ibid., pp. 78, 40, 96, 90, 41, 83, 51, 30.

43. Ibid., pp. 29, 84.

44. Ibid., pp. 89, 95.

45. See Joyce Carol Oates, "*The Picture of Dorian Gray:* Wilde's Parable of the Fall," *Critical Inquiry* 7 (Winter 1980): 419–28.

46. H. G. Wells, *The Time Machine* (1895; repr., New York: Berkley Books, 1982), pp. 49, 83.

47. Henrik Ibsen, *Ghosts,* in *Four Great Plays by Henrik Ibsen,* trans. R. Farquaharson Sharp (New York: Bantom Books, 1959), p. 99.

48. Michael Mayer, *Ibsen: A Biography* (New York: Doubleday & Co., 1971), pp. 657–59. See also Michael Egan, *Ibsen: The Critical Heritage* (London: Routledge & Kegan Paul, 1972).

49. Thomas Hardy, *Jude the Obscure* (Harmondsworth: Penguin Books, 1978), p. 42. All subsequent references to this novel are to this edition and are cited parenthetically by page number in the text.

50. Jane H. Clapperton, *A Vision of the Future* (London: Swan Sonnenschein, 1904), pp. 263–64.

51. Letter to Edmund Gosse, Nov. 30, 1895, in *The Collected Letters of Thomas Hardy,* ed. Richard L. Purdy and Michael Millgate (Oxford: Clarendon Press, 1980), 2:99.

52. Savage, *Insanity,* p. 22.

53. Havelock Ellis, "Concerning *Jude the Obscure,*" *Savoy Magazine,* Oct. 6, 1896, repr. in R. G. Cox, *Thomas Hardy: The Critical Heritage* (London: Routledge & Kegan Paul, 1970), p. 307.

54. See, for example, the review of *Jude* by Margaret Oliphant, "The Anti-Marriage League," *Blackwood's Magazine* 159 (Jan. 1896): 135–49.

55. Quoted in Sandra M. Gilbert and Susan Gubar, *The Madwoman in the Attic* (New Haven: Yale University Press, 1979), p. 3.

56. Havelock Ellis, "Thomas Hardy's Novels," *Westminster Review* (Apr. 1883), repr. in Cox, *Thomas Hardy,* p. 104.

57. See Patricia Stubbs, *Women and Fiction: Feminism and the Novel, 1880–1920* (New York: Barnes & Noble, 1979), p. 120.

58. H. Rider Haggard, *She* (1887; repr., New York: Airmont Classics Series, 1967), pp. 28, 76. I am indebted for the development of these ideas about Haggard to the insights and questions of the Princeton University graduate students in my seminar "Gender and Literary Theory," Fall 1984, especially those of Wayne Koestenbaum and Carol Barash.

59. Christabel Pankhurst, *The Great Scourge and How to End It* (London: David Nutt, 1913), pp. 133, 124.

60. Siegfried Sassoon, *Siegfried's Journey* (London: Faber & Faber, 1945), p. 30. For the theme of syphilis in relation to modern war-literature, see Mark Spilka, "Hemingway, Jones, and Kipling: Good Soldiers Three" (Paper presented at the Modern Language Association Annual Convention, Washington, D.C., Dec. 1984).

 *Mark Seltzer*

The Naturalist Machine

In these pages I will be concerned with a cluster of anxieties, at once sexual, economic, and aesthetic, that seems to be generated in the late nineteenth-century "naturalist" novel. More specifically, I will be considering an insistent anxiety about production and generation—generation of lives, powers, and representations—that marks this fiction. If, as the industrialist Cedarquist observes in Frank Norris's *The Octopus,* "the great word of this nineteenth century has been Production," production, both mechanical and biological, also troubles the naturalist novel at every point.[1] I want to suggest that the achievement of the naturalist novel appears at least in part in the devising of a counter-model of generation that incorporates and works to manage these linked, although not at all equivalent, problems of production and reproduction. The counter-model is what might be called the naturalist machine. Although I would argue that such a model operates in a wide range of naturalist texts, I want for the moment to take most of my examples from the work of the American novelist who most conspicuously and compulsively displays both these anxieties about generation and the aesthetic machine designed to manage them—Frank Norris.

I

Near the end of *The Octopus,* the railroad agent and speculator S. Berman is buried alive beneath a "living stream" of wheat, "this dreadful substance that was neither solid nor fluid" (2:353). The logic of such a fate is clear enough; it is explicitly represented as a productive or hyperproductive nature's revenge on what Norris throughout presents as the unnatural and nonproductive abuses of the speculator. If Berman is bodily, as the speculator Curtis Jadwin in Norris's *The Pit* is financially, buried by a flood of wheat, this is a sort of turn of nature on the speculator who attempts to appropriate or corner her living produce. But such a homeopathic logic fails to account for a somewhat different sort of uneasiness that "this dreadful substance" presents.

Just before this "inevitable" (2:355) end of the speculator, Berman discusses the terms of his deal in wheat with one of his agents. "This deal is peculiar," he observes, "it's a queer, mixed up deal." What is "queer" about the deal, it would seem, is its direct, unmediated character. "I'm not selling to any middleman," Berman explains: "I've got to have some hand in shipping this stuff myself" (2:328). But this exclusion of—or what the rancher Magnus Derrick earlier calls "stranding" of—the middleman turns out to be a little more complicated. Berman claims that he is "acting direct," but in fact, as he goes on to say, he's "acting direct with these women people," with a "lot of women people up in the city" who have contracted for the wheat as part of a project to relieve a famine in Asia (2:327).[2] What relation do the middlemen, on the one side, and the "women people," on the other, have to the logistics of production in the novel?

The Octopus, as I have indicated, invokes a traditional "agrarianist" opposition of producer and speculator or middleman, but such an opposition is not consistent with the account of production that the novel ultimately supports.[3] Not surprisingly, this account is articulated by the railroad titan Shelgrim, the novel's middleman par excellence. Shelgrim's reply to Presley's protest against the railroad's usurpation of the ranches and their wheat is in part a self-exonerating appeal to an invisible hand guiding the economy: "Where there is a demand sooner or later there will be a supply. . . . Blame conditions not men" (2:285). The ideological character of such a defense is evident. But Shelgrim's defense goes a bit further, in a manner that both more effectively threatens the opposition between producer and speculator that grounds Presley's protest, and concisely enunciates what Norris ends by endorsing as the "larger view" (2:361): "Try to believe this—to begin with—*that railroads build themselves.* . . . Mr. Derrick, does he grow his wheat? The Wheat grows itself. What does he count for? Does he supply the force?" (2:285). Crucially, by the logic of this larger view, there are no producers at all: all are middlemen, equally subject to or carriers of uncontrollable forces. One consequence of such a view is, of course, a radical emptying of the category of production— the very category that the social-economic "protest" the novel might be seen to embody centrally requires.

Yet, if production does not have a secure place in Norris's economic theory, the novel does offer an account of the "enigma of growth" and "mystery of creation" (2:343). *The Octopus* offers in fact *two* competing accounts of the force of production and generation. On the one side, and not unexpectedly, there is the mother, at once "the crown of motherhood . . . the beauty of the perfect woman" and the mother-land, "palpitating with the desire of reproduction" in the "hidden tumult of its womb" (2:215, 1:122), "the great earth, the mother, after its period of reproduction, its pains of labour, delivered of the fruit of its loins, [sleeping] the sleep of exhaustion in the infinite repose of the colossus" (1:123, 2:342-43). On the other, Norris represents the technology of the steam machine, "the jarring, jolting, trembling machine . . . the heroic embrace of a multitude of iron hands, gripping deep into the brown, warm flesh of the land" (1:124-25). These twinned representations of generative power—the machine and the mother—are suspended in relation to each other in the novel, as linked but competing principles of creation.

Norris's representation of steam power as generative, in *The Octopus* and throughout his work, participates in a more general field of middle and later nineteenth-century discourses on the procreative force of the machine. As Perry Miller has argued,

in the American representation of steam power in this period—
"the pure white jet that fecundates America"—the "imagery
frequently becomes, probably unconsciously, sexual, and so be-
trays how in this mechanistic orgasm modern America was conceived."[4] Such an association of steam power and generation—
what writers of the midcentury described as "the marriage of
water and heat" that inseminates the "body of the continent"—
is part of a larger celebration of technology by which Americans
viewed the machine, and especially the steam engine and dynamo
or "generator," as a "replacement for the human body."[5] More
precisely, this "replacement" registers also a displaced competition between rival sexual forces, between what Norris, for instance, calls the "two world-forces, the elemental Male and
Female" (1:125).

The nineteenth-century obstetrician and gynecologist Augustus Kinsley Gardner opens his lecture *The History of the Art of
Midwifery* (1852) by concisely invoking these two rival principles of generation: "From the foundation of the world man has
been born of women; and notwithstanding that his inventive
genius has discovered steam, the great Briareus of the nineteenth
century, and has harnessed him to his chariot, and sends light-
ning to do his bidding over the almost boundless extent of the
world, yet we cannot hope that any change may be affected in
this particular."[6] Despite or "notwithstanding" the rhetorical
disclaimers, it is not hard to see that Gardner's purpose, here
and elsewhere, is to "replace" female generative power with an
alternative practice, at once technological and male. As Graham
Barker-Benfield argues in his study of attitudes toward women
and sexuality in Victorian America, one of the governing impulses promoting the medicalization of women and childbirth
in the nineteenth century was the desire "to take charge of the
procreative function in all of its aspects."[7] And one of the
markers in this takeover was an attack on female midwifery and
the substitution of the professional and male technology of
obstetrics. This amounted to, in effect, not merely an increasing

male management of procreation but also a revaluing of the midwife's position in relation to reproduction. That is, if the obstetrician replaces the (female) midwife, his confiscation of the generative function places him as the governing middleman of reproduction, and governing precisely because of his position as middleman. And if Norris's image of the earth mother is centrally obstetrical—the mother "delivered," after the pains of labor—this delivery, by the iron "knives" of the steam harvester, represents, I want to suggest, a collateral reassertion of the middleman—again, the position of all men in Norris's account—in the process of production.

It is tempting to read this revaluation of the middle*man* as a compensatory male response to a threatening female productivity, and, as Barker-Benfield, among others, has suggested, this is certainly a significant part of the story. But the notion of, and promotion of, a rivalry between "male" and "female" forces, and the consequent underwriting of what appears as an absolute differentiation of gender powers and "principles," may in fact function as ways of managing the anxieties about production I have been sketching. Put another way, we must consider the ways in which difference itself may be produced and deployed as a strategy of control and as part of a more general economy of bodies and powers. One of the narrative tactics that supports this economy is the displacement or rewriting of generative power, and one of the supports of such tactics is the resolutely abstract account of "force" that governs the naturalist text.

The passage on the earth mother's delivery is, in characteristic Norris fashion, repeated several times in the novel. The final repetition is quickly succeeded by two remarkable rewritings of the force of (re)production. The mother initially appears to extradite men from a place in what Norris calls "the explanation of existence": "men were nothings, mere animalcules." The negation of male power is evident.[8] But through the double operation of negation and reinvestment that I have already noted in Norris's explanations of production, a curious revaluation follows. If the titanic mother reduces men to "nothings," "for one second Presley could go one step further": "Men were naught, death was naught, life was naught; FORCE only existed— FORCE that brought men into the world, FORCE that crowded them out of it to make way for the succeeding generation, FORCE that made the wheat grow, FORCE that garnered it from the soil to give place to the succeeding crop" (2:343). The colossal mother is thus rewritten as a machine of force that brings men into the world, "the symphony of reproduction" as "the colossal pendulum of an almighty machine." And crucially, if the mother is merely a "carrier" of force, the mother herself is merely a medium—midwife and middleman—of the force of generation.

Such a capitalizing on force as a counter to female generativity in particular and to anxieties about generation and production in general may help to explain, at least in part, the appeals to highly abstract conceptions of force in the emphatically "male" genre of naturalism.[9] More specifically, and despite the instabilities and contradictions in the naturalist conception of force, it does not take much interpretive pressure to see that this discourse of force, crucial to the naturalist style of power, is essentially the discourse of thermodynamics.[10] I am referring not merely to the centrality of steam power in the naturalist text (preeminently Zola's) but also to the "laws" that govern what I have called the naturalist machine. The two fundamental principles of thermodynamics—the law of conservation and the law of dissipation—operate, I want to argue, both thematically and formally in the naturalist narrative. The pertinence of the second law—positing the irreversible degradation of usable energy in any system and hence an inevitable systemic degeneration—to the naturalist doctrine of degeneration is immediately evident, and I will be discussing this "application" of the second law in the section following. But here I am more concerned with some surprising consequences of the first law for the naturalist problematic of production. Stated simply, the first law of thermodynamics, the law of conservation, posits that matter and energy may be converted and exchanged but can neither be created nor destroyed. As Henry Adams puts it in *The Degradation of the Democratic Dogma,* in which he details and applies a thermodynamic theory of history, there is "incessant transference and conversion," but "nothing was created, nothing was destroyed."[11] Conversion without creation is the thermodynamic conception of force.

The significance of such a conception of force is not hard to detect: the opposition of conversion to creation forms the basis of late nineteenth-century theories of production. In his *Theory of the Leisure Class* (1899), for instance, Thorstein Veblen, not unlike Norris, offers essentially an agrarianist contrast between "industry," which involves "the effort to create a new thing," and the nonproductive or wasteful activities of what Veblen calls "exploit" and "conspicuous consumption," which he defines as "the conversion to his own ends of energies previously directed to some other end by another agent."[12] Such a difference between creation of a new thing and mere conversion of energy, Veblen immediately adds, "coincides with a difference between the sexes."[13] This "coincidence" figures centrally in what is certainly the most familiar American naturalist treatment of the relation between thermodynamics and sexual production, Henry Adams's treatment of the virgin and the dynamo in *The Education of Henry Adams.*

Adams's text repeats Veblen's opposition of industry and conversion, but with inverse valuation. Adams's meditation on the power of the Virgin takes place, of course, in the Gallery of Machines at the Great Exposition at Paris in 1900. Adams relates that he "ignored almost the whole industrial exhibit," attending instead to the steam engine and dynamo. What these machines perform is a conversion of matter and energy: "To him, the dynamo was but an ingenious channel for conveying somewhere the heat latent in a few tons of poor coal." This power of "interconversion of forms," "endless displacement," and ceaseless "exchange" defines the "wholly new" force of the dynamo. This new power is also perfectly in line with what Adams represents as the final giving way, in the 1890s, of a "simply industrial" economy of production to a "capitalist system" and "machine" ruled by the laws of conversion and exchange.[14]

On the levels of the machine and the body both, Adams's economy is thermodynamic. As he concisely states in his "Letter to American Teachers of History" (1910), "man is a thermodynamic mechanism."[15] And Adams's treatment of the reproductive power of the Virgin offers not finally an alternative to but an extension of this dynamic. The Virgin "was reproduction," Adams observes, "the greatest and most mysterious of energies." She is also "the animated dynamo," the living generator. If the dynamo is an "ingenious channel" of conversion, the Virgin is a "channel of force."[16] The Virgin, not unlike Dreiser's Sister Carrie, who explicitly represents, at the close of the novel, a "medium" and "carrier" of force, and not unlike Norris's "mother," the conveyer of the force that brought men into the world, is a thermodynamic mechanism, a converter of power. In Norris's formulation, "Nature was, then, a gigantic engine" (2:286).

This is enough to indicate, at least provisionally, part of what I suggest is at the back of Norris's rewriting of production and some of the implications and effects of that revision. But as I earlier indicated, the logic of the passage I began by considering is yet more complicated. The translation of earth mother into force is immediately succeeded by yet another explanation of generation, an explanation that goes even a step further. As if the leveling appeal to an abstract and disembodied "FORCE" fails to reinvest the role of men in production, this account of force is followed by a startling reembodiment. This new and miraculous body recovers not merely a male power of production but also projects the autonomy of that power. The "almighty machine" that displaces the colossal mother is a channel of energy. This machine, however, takes on a strikingly different form: it is a generator of "primordial energy flung out from the hand of the Lord God himself, immortal, calm, infinitely strong." One might say that creation, in Norris's final explanation, is the work of an inexhaustible masturbator, spilling his seed on the ground, the product of a mechanistic and miraculous onanism. The third term in Norris's triptych of mother, force, and onanist-machine places power back into the hands of the immortal and autonomous male technology of generation.

Such an invocation of an autonomous and masturbatory economy of production characterizes the discourse of naturalism generally, and anticipates, for instance, Dreiser's portrayal, in the "trilogy of desire" novels, of the powerful financier, Frank Cowperwood, whose motto—"I satisfy myself"—and notion of procreation—"he liked . . . the idea of self-duplication"—closely resemble the attributes of Norris's god.[17] But it is necessary to note that the very multiplicity of accounts of production that Norris offers, the familiar sublimations and personifications, the "miraculous" explanations of the "miracle of creation"—all indicate the unstable displacements of production in Norris's account. They indicate as well how this very multiplicity and instability may ultimately function as a flexible and polyvalent textual mechanism of relays, conversions, and "crisis" management—as, in fact, a thermodynamic that forms part of the textual mechanism itself.

Moreover, it is necessary to note that the three-part rewriting of reproduction that I have focused on is abruptly interpolated into the "plot" of the novel. The question remains: How does the autonomous and miraculous or "miraculated" production traced here operate in the production and genealogy of Norris's narrative itself?[18] Or, from a somewhat different perspective, how does such a management of production structure the naturalist narrative machine? I take up this question in some detail in the following discussion of Norris's *Vandover and the Brute*.

But I want to close this account of *The Octopus* by suggesting at least some of the more local "stories" that constitute the novel's techniques of generation and invention of a technology of generation that is also a technology of power. Put simply, what unites these stories is the desire to project an alternative to biological reproduction, to displace the threat posed by the "women people" (the reduction of men to "mere animalcules" in the process of procreation) and to devise a countermode of reproduction (the naturalist machine). One indicator of such a desire is the novel's scandalized representation of "that dreadful substance that was neither solid nor fluid," the scandal posed by "seed," in all its forms, in the novel. The aversion to both women and seed is clearest in the figure who is, interestingly enough, the novel's primary exponent of the technocratic New Agriculture, the wheat-grower Annixter. What above all characterizes Annixter is, on the one side, his horror of what he calls "female girls," and on the other, his horror of a substance he calls "sloop," a "thick, gruel-like, colorless mixture"—"slimy, disgusting stuff"—that he finds in his bed (1:98, 117). Annixter's "hereditary" aversion to semen, and his singular way of cursing—"he is a *pip*"—together with his uneasiness about the "idea" of the woman, make his antibiological bias hard to miss. The "solution," in the terms that the novel presents, would be a nonbiological and miraculated production that circumvents these threats and projects an autonomous (and male) technique of creation. Such a solution is most readily apparent in the two "love stories" in the novel: Vanamee's romance with Angéle, I and II, and Annixter's romance with his milkmaid, Hilma.

The sheer perversity of the Vanamee-Angéle story provides an almost diagrammatic instance of what might be called the double discourse of the novel, a double writing by which (re)production is displaced or disavowed and rewritten in another register. On one level, the "facts" can be quickly summarized. The shepherd Vanamee meets his sixteen-year-old lover Angéle each night in the churchyard. One night he is anticipated by a mysterious stranger, Angéle is raped, and dies in giving birth to the consequent child ("her death at the moment of her child's birth" [1:45]). Sixteen years later Vanamee resumes his love affair, with Angéle's daughter and exact double. What is most perverse about the story, however, is not its violent and even murderous treatment of sexuality and procreation, but the violence of its symmetries and the urgent translation of these events into the miraculous terms of what Norris calls "romance."

In his representation of "FORCE," Norris translates the "mystery of creation" as the "miracle of re-creation" (2:343), a revision that converts life and death into mere epiphenomenal embodiments of force, cyclical and substitutable repetitions, reproduction as miraculous re-production. Similarly, Vanamee's mysterious and telepathic calling back of Angéle from the dead is a miracle of re-creation, a simple replacement of daughter for mother: "Angéle or Angéle's daughter, it was all one with him. It was She" (2:106). What such a replacement achieves is a circumvention of both the "defilement" of Angéle's sexuality and the "birth" of her daughter. Vanamee's "mysterious" power of telepathy symmetrically counters what is repeatedly described in the novel as "the mystery of the Other" (1:45), a mystery that ultimately points not merely to the otherness of the unknown rapist but also to the alterity of sexual procreation in the novel. Stated simply, the calling forth of the new Angéle— from, of course, the Seed Ranch—translates reproduction into reincarnation, and such a reincarnation collates exactly with the logistics of production I have already traced. "Angéle," Norris writes, "was realized in the Wheat" (2:347). In his manuscript notes for the novel, Norris is even more precise: "Angéle is the wheat."[19] One might say that Angéle, like the wheat, grows herself, though—again like the wheat—her manifestation or delivery is in other hands. If the "trembling" steam plow "gripping deep into the brown, warm flesh of the land" "seemed to reproduce itself in [Vanamee's] finger-tips" (2:125, 124),

Vanamee's reincarnative power offers finally an emphatically personified and personifying technique of nonbiological and autonomous reproduction, or what amounts to a mechanical reproduction of persons.

Hilma Annixter (née Tree) presents a rather different problem for the novel's reworking of generation, since Hilma represents above all a power of maternity, albeit a power miraculated as "radiance of the unseen crown of motherhood glowing from her forehead" (2:215). The threat that Hilma poses is apparent. Not only does she possess the typically Amazonian body of Norris's mother-women, she also exerts an unsettling control over Annixter. Exercising the "influence of a wife, who was also a mother" (2:209), Hilma literally reforms Annixter, and in a manner that, as should by now be clear, makes for a dangerous vulnerability: "She's made a man of me," Annixter explains, "I was a machine before" (2:180). Not surprisingly, the scene of Annixter's death is juxtaposed to the scene celebrating Hilma's maternity.[20] But if Hilma dutifully miscarries after Annixter's murder, I suggest that the novel's strategy for containing and appropriating the power that Hilma represents takes a somewhat different and more surreptitious form.

Norris's description of Hilma, and more particularly, of her hair, which "seemed almost to have a life of its own, almost Medusa-like" (1:80), reinforces the sense of the milkmaid's unmanning fecundity.[21] But the description invokes as well another and startling cluster of associations: "Deep in between the coils and braids it was of a bitumen brownness, but in the sunlight it vibrated with a sheen like tarnished gold" (1:80). Hilma's hair, bitumen and gold, is something of a mine. What relation might there be between mining and the logistics of generation in the novel?

The Octopus at several points contrasts mining and farming, and in terms directly related to its account of generation. Whereas farming, as we have seen, involves "the elemental passion of Male and Female," mining has a different character. As Annixter protests, "Derrick [the former gold-miner turned rancher] thinks he's still running his mine, and that the same principles will apply to getting grain out of the earth as to getting gold" (1:26). The difference between getting grain and getting gold is a difference between those who "husband" (1:61) their resources and those who "had no love for their land . . . were not attached to the soil" (2:14). And the difference between husbanders and miners is the difference between a loving "embrace" of the earth and violent extraction, "get[ting] the guts out of your land" (1:26), or as Norris depicts mining in *McTeague,* reaching into "the very entrails of the earth . . . boring into the vitals . . . tearing away great yellow gravelly scars in the flanks of them, sucking their blood, extracting gold."[22]

For Norris, as he represents it in *McTeague,* the body of the earth is at once female and "untamed": "she is a vast, unconquered brute . . . savage, sullen, and magnificently indifferent to man." "But," he immediately adds, "there were men in these mountains" (213), and the activities of these men, explicitly allied to the technologies of mining, to the force and "black smoke" of the steam machines, constitute a twofold assault on the mother earth by her "progeny": a violent ingestion and assimilation and an extraction from her "vitals" that resembles a violent obstetrics. Nor is Norris's representation of mining at all anomalous in this period. In his popular history of California, *The Sunset Land* (1870), for instance, the Reverend John Todd, a minister who also wrote student manuals governing sexual behavior, contrasts mining, which he calls "the unnatural creation of property" to the more natural creations of agriculture. He notes as well that the eagerness of newly arrived California gold-seekers was so great that "infants were turned out of cradles, that the cradles might be used for washing gold." Todd may be confusing the miner's sieve, called a cradle, with the infant's cradle, but the confusion itself is perhaps significant. (Todd, we may note, officiated at what was called the "wedding" of track that formed the first transcontinental railroad, and

thereafter wore a wedding ring made from the gold of the linking "golden spike.") Such a confusion is perhaps shared by Norris's Trina McTeague, for instance, who weeps over the empty
bag and box that had contained her gold coins "as other women
weep over a dead baby's shoe" (198). Todd, among others, frequently sees the extraction of wealth from the "bosom of
mother earth" as a counterimage of procreation, and indeed
contraposes such male "unnatural" creation to a threatening female generativity.[23]

The contrast between mining and farming provides a final
instance of the novel's rewriting of production. The extraction
of gold from the very entrails of the mother earth is ultimately
a species of obstetrics that can dispense with the women-people,
and indeed with the body and its dreadful substance, altogether.
Seen this way, gold-mining extracts value directly from what
Marx called "the womb of capital itself."[24] And *The Octopus*,
making capital of its instabilities and exigencies, provides a virtual
map of the crises of production in the late nineteenth century, and of the representations invented to manage these crises.

II

I have to this point deferred considering the aesthetic consequences of the naturalist mechanics of generation I have been
indicating. The insistent displacements and ceaseless conversions
of force in Norris's texts might be seen to register a thermodynamic technology of power. What remains to be considered are
the ways in which such a technology is reinvented and promoted
by the techniques of the naturalist narrative itself, and the consequences, at once aesthetic and political, of such an assimilation of the practices of the body in a general and comprehensive
social technology of power.

The production of works of art, throughout Norris's texts,
takes the form of a process of gestation. In *The Octopus,* for

instance, the poet Presley sees his projected work "germinating from within" (1:6), as a sort of pregnancy: "the desire of creation, of composition, grew big within him. . . . Not for a long time had he 'felt his poem,' as he called this sensation" (1:42). But if such a connection between composition and gestation is familiar enough in romantic and postromantic aesthetics, what makes for the ultimate *in*effectuality of Presley's art is the novel's invention of a counter-principle of reproduction. Presley's art fails not merely because, as the railroad titan Shelgrim points out, his poem—about labor—simply imitates the painting he "took the idea from" (2:283) rather than directly reproduces "life," but also because Presley's art cannot compete with the technology that Shelgrim represents: "Again and again, he brought up against the railroad, that stubborn iron barrier against which his romance shattered itself to froth and disintegrated, flying spume" (1:10). Presley's labor remains "abortive" (2:85)—filled with "terrible formless shapes, vague figures . . . monstrous" (1:8)—or simply onanistic, because his romantic "spume" cannot compete with the inexhaustible and regulated "white jet" of the steam engine. What the naturalist aesthetic requires, then, is a principle of generation that incorporates rather than opposes the machine: in short, a mechanics that forms part of its very textuality. The discovery and operation of such a machine is the subject of Norris's *Vandover and the Brute,* a novel written before *The Octopus,* but not published until 1914, and a novel centrally about processes of generation, and more particularly, degeneration.

Early in the novel, the young Vandover looks through the books of his father's library for the dollar bill that the "Old Gentleman" had "at one time misplaced between the leaves of some one of the great tomes."[25] What Vandover finds instead is a long article on "Obstetrics" in an old *Encyclopaedia Britannica,* an article "profusely illustrated with old-fashioned plates and steel engravings. He read it from beginning to end" (10). A little later on, he finds "in the same library" a "Home

Book of Art," illustrated with sentimental and idealized pictures of girls and women, "ideal 'Heads' " (12–13). This juxtaposition, and network, of obstetrics, capital, and a certain style of art initiate and direct the "plot" of the novel.

For one thing, the novel foregrounds an exact equivalence between Vandover's "reckless spending" of the property he inherits from his father and the accelerating process of his degeneration into "the brute." But what at first might appear as a simple "opposition" between proper saving, on one side, and spendthrift dissipation, on the other, turns out to be somewhat more complicated. Vandover's money, and in particular the bonds or "4 per cents" represent the regulated productions of what is indeed a womb of capital: the bonds, "faithfully brooding over his eighty-nine hundred in the dark of the safety deposit drawer, would bring forth their little quota of twenty-three with absolute certainty" (171). Far from being simply at odds with such a process of production, Vandover's degeneration, precipitated by his discovery of the obstetrics article, involves not merely his reversion into the brute but more precisely another and monstrous process of gestation. If "little by little the brute had grown" (215), this growth, "knitted into him now, fibre for fibre" (277), swelling within the core of his body, "that fatal central place where the brute had its lair" (219), and "feeding its abominable hunger" on "his very self" (30, 316), is a strikingly perverse case in obstetrics. I am suggesting then that if these two economies—of saving or conserving and of dissipating or degeneration—seem to be directly at odds, they are in fact linked by the novel's account of generation. I want to suggest further that these two economies constitute the two governing principles, at once linked and contradictory, of a more general economy of reproduction in the novel, a general economy that functions, moreover, precisely by way of its contradictions. What makes this contradictory economy *operational* is the complex force that Norris calls "the brute."

Vandover sets against the monstrous generation of the brute

the "desire of art [that] had grown big within him" (112). The artistic "new life" (116) he desires, as the circumstances of the discovery of the "Home Book of Art" imply, is a projected counter to generation and degeneration both—"Vandover the true man, Vandover the artist . . . not Vandover the lover of women" (112). But Vandover's artistic new life reinvents, on several not entirely compatible levels, the very obstetrics he attempts to evade. Turning to his art as an idealized mode of generation, Vandover discovers in horror that the lines he draws have "no life," that in fact these lines were "those of a child just learning to draw" (224). What "grew under his charcoal" instead were "grotesque and meaningless shapes, mocking caricatures" (225): "Once more certain shapes and figures were born upon his canvas, but they were no longer the true children of his imagination, they were no longer his own; they were changelings, grotesque abortions. It was as if the brute in him, like some malicious witch, had stolen away the true offspring of his mind, putting in their place these deformed dwarfs, its own hideous spawn" (229). Vandover explicitly sees this "death" of his art as an abortion, or as the "death of a child of his," and the agent of death or abortion, this midwife or witch-mother, is the very brute gestating within him. The monstrous gestation of the brute is at the same time an obstetrics-in-reverse. Not merely does Vandover's sketch resemble that of a child learning to draw, but his degradation is literally a reversed generation. The growth of the brute is also a return to the scene of birth—"he had become a little child again . . . still near to the great white gates of life" (214). And if Vandover turns to his art as an attempt to "deliver himself by his own exertions" (219), this attempt at self-delivery, in the novel's logic of generation, places Vandover in the places at once of mother, fetus, and obstetrician.

The painting that Vandover is attempting is a sentimental death scene, "The Last Enemy," and his art is still under the influence of "the melodrama of the old English 'Home Book of Art'" (64). But his aesthetic is usurped and twisted by the malicious agency of the brute, and the huge (and "life-size") canvas on which he attempts to body it forth—"the stretcher, blank, and untouched" of "heavy cream-white twill" (223)— becomes the scene of a perverse *accouchement*. Finally, and above all, the brute itself embodies not merely a counter-principle of generation but a counter-aesthetic as well: an aesthetic of caricature, monstrosity, and deformity, an aesthetic of genesis as *de*generation—that is, the aesthetic of the naturalist novel. Stated as simply as possible, the brute is the generative principle of naturalism.

From one point of view, *Vandover and the Brute* maps a process of degradation; from another, a process of generation. What links these apparently opposed processes is the agency of the brute. A conservative aesthetic of regulation is embodied in the central objet d'art in the novel, Vandover's "famous stove," a little machine decorated with pictures depicting the punishment of excess and dissipation, which he carefully tends and adjusts, "the life and soul" of the place (182). Incorporating a regulative aesthetic with a thermodynamic apparatus, the stove might be taken to emblematize, like his father's safe, the ethics of regulation and conservation that Vandover opposes to the brute.[26] But as I have already suggested, such an opposition between conserving and regulating, at one extreme, and the dissipations of the brute, at the other, cannot finally account for the contradictory force that the brute represents. Vandover's resistances to degradation effectively end with the wreck of the steamship *Mazatlan,* a wreck that forecloses his attempts to escape his degeneration. But if, like Vandover's stove and the "steady" and "cheerful" smokestacks that mark the topography of Norris's (and also Zola's) novels, the steam engine represents a regulated economy of power, the engine is at the same time a "strange huge living creature," an "enormous brute," and its ultimate wreck, the "death" of the brute (135). It appears that the brute is at once a principle of dissipation and of generation—a principle of death and also the life and soul of the novel. The brute operates a contradictory aesthetic allied throughout to the workings of the machine. A closer examination of the "laws" of that machine can perhaps help to clarify the rules of this double discourse and the way in which these contradictions function within a larger system of regulation.

One of the most striking indices of the naturalist aesthetic, as we have seen, is just this close link between generation and degradation, or, more simply, between reproduction and death. If such a linking seems somewhat startling, it in fact functions as one of the basic assumptions of late nineteenth-century theories of reproduction. In *The Octopus* the "return" of Angéle clearly invokes such a connection of generation and dissipation: "Life out of death, eternity rising from out of dissolution . . . the seed dying, rotting, and corrupting in the earth; rising again in life . . . *that which thou sowest is not quickened except it die*" (2:106). Norris's argument here most likely draws on the work of Joseph Le Conte, the religion-oriented evolutionist whose class Norris attended at the University of California, Berkeley in 1892–93. In his essay, "Correlation of Vital with Chemical and Physical Processes" (1875), for instance, Le Conte's thesis is that all life is "generated by decomposition." The seed, for example, "always loses weight in germination; it *cannot* develop unless it is in part consumed; 'it is not quickened except it die.'" In short, Le Conte maintains that "the law of death necessitates the law of reproduction."[27]

The laws Le Conte appeals to here are thermodynamic, and the economy of decomposition without loss he invokes is an explicit mapping of the laws of conservation and of dissipation onto vital processes, a direct application of thermodynamic conceptions of force to the body. As Le Conte repeatedly observes, "the prime object in the body, as in the steam-engine, is [transfer of] force."[28] One consequence of such an application of thermodynamic to vital processes in the late nineteenth century was a radical reconceptualization of the biology of

sexual reproduction. This rewriting involved not merely a correlation of genesis and degeneration, but also the invention of a
model of sexual difference based on thermodynamic concepts.
The deployment of this model is perhaps clearest in the work of
the Scottish biologist and sociologist, Patrick Geddes.

In the highly influential *Evolution of Sex* (1889), Geddes and
J. Arthur Thomson propose a biological explanation for differences between male and female social and ethical roles, an explanation based on what they see as an absolute difference
between the cellular biology of the sexes. Opposing Darwin's
explanation of sexual differentiation, Geddes and Thomson
hold that, for instance, "males are stronger, handsomer, or more
emotional," not through a process of natural selection, but
"simply because they are males." What differentiates male and
female is the cellular metabolism that predominates in each.
Male cells are "katabolic," that is, characterized by expenditure
and breakdown, whereas female cells are "anabolic," conservative and constructive. "Males live at a loss . . . females, on the
other hand, live at a profit." By this logic, males embody the
second law of thermodynamics—the law of dissipation; females
the first—the law of conservation. A thermodynamic biology
thus underwrites a political economy of sexual difference, and,
more specifically, a typology of genders that precisely corre-
sponds to naturalist typologies of character—for instance, the
opposition between McTeague's reckless spending and Trina's
"instinct" for saving, in Norris's *McTeague.* But Geddes and
Thomson's account is perhaps most interesting for our purposes
in the rather remarkable consequences of their theory for the
explanation of reproduction they offer. Geddes and Thomson,
like Le Conte, focus on the "close connection between reproduction and death," and what follows from this close connection is the notion that "the two facts of reproduction and
death . . . may both be described as katabolic crises." And
since reproduction in this account is a katabolic process, an
unlooked-for dividend that this thermodynamics of the body

ultimately entails is that generation—for Geddes as for Norris—is by definition a male process.[29]

These evolutionary accounts of generation help to clarify what I have called the double discourse of the brute in the naturalist novel, the manner in which apparently conflicting processes of generation and degradation operate within a more comprehensive technology of regulation. More generally, these accounts point to the late nineteenth-century double discourse by which the "contradictory" registers of the body and the machine are "floated" in relation to each other and coordinated within a general economy of power. I have elsewhere attempted to outline how such a "system of flotation" and conversion functions in late nineteenth-century social and novelistic discourses and practices, and the manner in which a circuit of exchange is established between, on the basis of and by way of, conflicting and differentiated practices.[30] What is gradually elaborated is a more or less efficient, more or less effective system of transformations and relays between "opposed" and contradictory registers—between public and private spaces; between social norms and private values; between work and world on the one side, and home and family on the other; between, more generally, "the economic" and "the sexual." A flexible mechanism of adjustment is established, intrinsically promoting a coordination of conflicting practices, while strategically preserving the differences between these practices. Conflicts are, in principle, conscripted into a "circular functionality" between, for instance, "the two registers of the production of goods and the production of producers (and consumers)."[31] Or, in terms of the naturalist logistics I have been considering, between the sievelike registers of the machine and the body. These new, or rather, newly inflected, strategies of regulation advertise the differences between public and private, and between economic and sexual domains, even as they reinforce and extend the lines of communication between them. But if each appears as the alternative to and sanctuary from the other, as the privileged site from which the other may be criticized and abjured, what these deployments of difference effectively obscure are precisely the links and relays progressively set in place "between" these opposed domains.

From this perspective, the utility and spreading of the thermodynamic model of force in the later nineteenth century become more intelligible. This scientifically sanctioned and flexibly generalizable model provided at once a system of transformation and exchange (a principle of conversion) and, in the relays, shifts, and contradictions that facilitate these exchanges, a system of crisis management (a deployment of difference). The discourse of thermodynamics provided a working model of a new mechanics and biomechanics of power. Moreover, I have been indicating that the transformational system that manages, and capitalizes on, these differences and conflicts between the sexual and the economic, between the body and the machine, is that field of practices that Michel Foucault has called the "biopolitical." Taking as its field of analysis a politics of the body and of the social body, such an analytic identifies a network of practices located "between the empty gesture of the voluntary and the inscrutable efficiency of the involuntary," and reexamines "the endless cleavage between politics and psychology" by focusing on the constitution of the subject as the subject of power.[32] What such an examination of the biopolitical dimension reveals is the subject's production at the point of intersection of sexual and economic practices and techniques; and what such a production of producers involves is not an ineradicable antinomy between "system" and "subject," between political economy and individual psychology, between anonymous technologies of power and gender-differentiated sexual "identities," but rather a set of exchanges operating between and by way of these antinomies, "choices," and differences. The point, finally, is not to collapse these differences, but to examine their mobility and also their tactical mobilization.

More specifically, I am suggesting that Geddes's theory of sexual difference culminates an attempt, taking off in the late eighteenth century, to provide a biological explanation and justification for gender inequalities. "What was decided among the prehistoric Protozoa," Geddes simply remarks, "cannot be annulled by an Act of Parliament."[33] But most significant in Geddes's account is the perfect fit between the *scientia sexualis* he provides and the power play it entails, the ways in which a thermodynamic technology of power invests and confiscates processes of life and of generation. Such a political economy of reproduction is a local move in a far more thoroughgoing movement over the course of the nineteenth century, a movement that involved the invention and dissemination of a regulative biopolitics. As the Reverend Josiah Strong observed in his popular *The Times and Young Men* (1901), "Evidently, getting the most good out of life, which is getting the most service into it, raises the problem of *The Body*."[34] The aim, as Strong observes elsewhere, is a "balance of power," a balance, as Strong's formula of "getting" and "servicing" indicates, between an ethos of production and an emergent culture of consumption. What is desired is an adjustment between conflicting practices, between a proper conservation of vital powers and the productive utilization of those powers. "The means of self-gratification," Strong insists, "must not outgrow the power of self-control," and more powerful technologies of production must be "accompanied by an increasing power of control."[35]

The focus of this practical and theoretical search for a balance of powers is "the body." One might point to the "medicalization" of late nineteenth-century American society, the rise of therapeutic practices, of eugenics, euthenics, "scientific motherhood," and "physical cultures," and also the rewritings of sexual biology and reproduction already considered. One might cite also William James's investigations of psychic and physical energies and economies, or the evolutionary biology of G. Stanley Hall, whose major work, *Adolescence* (1904), posits a

curriculum for the psychic and physical growth of the male
adolescent, a process of growth that draws on but ultimately
moves beyond the nurturing powers of a miraculated "all
mother." (Indeed, Hall's maternal "moon goddess" and her displaced role in generation and growth provide a virtual abstract
of the "miraculated" generation that we have examined.) The
development of these tactics for dealing with "the problem of
the body" has recently begun to be documented, and I want
here merely to indicate the larger field in which the technologies of generation I have focused on function.[36] What I want to
consider finally, and from a somewhat different perspective, are
the ways in which the evolutionary theory allied to these technologies extends such a politics of the body and, collaterally,
the ways in which the naturalist novel itself relays these tactics
of control.

III

In *Surveiller et punir,* Foucault suggests that the "two great
'discoveries' of the eighteenth century—the progress of societies
and the geneses of individuals—were perhaps correlative with
the new techniques of power." Such disciplinary techniques, he
argues, require bodies at once regulated and productive, and
operate, in part, by making use of and assimilating the "genesis"
and evolution of the individual within a general tactic of subjec-
tion. The discoveries of evolution and of individual genesis
make possible the articulation of a practice of domination that
involves a "new way of administering time" that is also a new
way of administering individuals, bodies, and populations. What
emerges is an "organic" economy of control linked to and taking hold of the organic evolution of individuals and societies
alike. Thus, Foucault suggests, "'Evolutive historicity,' as it
was then constituted—and so profoundly that it is still self-
evident for many today—is bound up with a mode of functioning

of power," a power that takes as its field of application "the 'dynamics' of continual evolutions."[37]

One of the social practices that underwrites such an administration of power in duration is the nineteenth-century novel, and more particularly the realist novel. The subject of the realist novel, stated very generally, is the internal genesis and evolution of character in society. The realist novel, through techniques of narrative surveillance, organic continuity, and deterministic progress, secures the intelligibility and supervision of individuals in an evolutionary and genetic narration. The linear continuities of the novel make for a "progress" that proceeds as an unfolding and generation of character and action that are always, at least ideally, consistent with their determining antecedents.[38] The naturalist novel involves a mutation 'in these techniques that consists also in a systematic and totalizing intensification of their effects. This mutation, again stated very generally, makes for functional shifts in emphasis—thematic and narrative shifts, for instance, from inheritance to heredity, from progress (as evolution) to recapitulation (as devolution), from histories of marriage and adultery to case histories of bodies, sexualities, and populations. Yet these differences themselves emphasize a significant continuity: if the realist novel resembles a time machine, the naturalist novel diagrammatically foregrounds, and maps in high relief, the evolutionary dynamics of this machinery.

Far from resisting the realist premises of genesis and generation, the naturalist aesthetic doctrines of determinism and degeneration systematically render explicit and reinforce these premises and the power-effects inscribed in them. Perhaps the most tendentious instance of such a narrative power play occurs, conveniently enough, near the opening of *Vandover and the Brute.* The novel begins by presenting scattered memories or "memory pictures" that from time to time return to Vandover's consciousness "absolutely independent of their importance" (3). The central picture is a scene in a train station, the locomotive "filling the place with a hideous clangor and with the smell of steam and of hot oil" (5). The scene involves the death of Vandover's mother, a death associated throughout the novel with the force of the steam engine. (This memory picture recurs, for instance, at the novel's pivotal point, the wreck of the steamship.) But if this connection between body and machine, as I have argued, governs Norris's mechanics of generation, Vandover himself "could remember nothing connectedly": "What he at first imagined to be the story of his life, on closer inspection turned out to be but a few disconnected incidents" (3). A few paragraphs into the novel, however, there is an abrupt shift in narrative mode. "In order to get at his life," Norris writes, "Vandover would have been obliged to collect these scattered memory pictures as best he could, rearrange them in some more orderly sequence . . . fill in the many gaps" (5). It is just such a move from disconnected pictures to sequential plotting that the novel at this point achieves, a taking over from Vandover that is also an explicit narrative takeover. This rearrangement in sequence engages the novel's relentless logic of devolution, the organic, genetic, and predetermined process of degeneration that Norris's narrative machine traces. Or, as Norris puts it in an essay on the art of the novel titled, neatly enough, "The Mechanics of Fiction," this move from picture to plot is what allows the "entire machinery to labour, full steam, ahead." The art of the novel, for Norris, is a "system of fiction mechanics"; his analogy for the defective novel is "the liner with hastily constructed boilers." And a proper mechanics of fiction involves the "systematizing" of discrete pictures into a segmented and connected series, into an organized and genetic narration: "The great story of the whole novel is told thus as it were in a series of pictures, the author supplying information as to what had intervened."[39] For Norris, the art of the novel is a mechanics of power.

Norris's mechanics of fiction concisely invokes and assimilates the technologies of power I have been considering. The techniques of the naturalist machine, its rewritings of production and deployments of a thermodynamic model, reinvent and relay late nineteenth-century social technologies of power and biopower. The achievement of the naturalist novel lies in the devising of a narrative machine that inscribes these technologies as part of its textual practice. In all, the naturalist novel manages late nineteenth-century "crises" of production by the invention of a flexible and totalizing machine of power. Suspending contradictory practices in relation to each other, and intrinsically promoting a coordination and adjustment of these practices, the naturalist machine operates through a double discourse by which the apparently opposed registers of the body and the machine are coordinated within a single technology of regulation.

NOTES

I want to thank Shirley Samuels and Ruth Bernard Yeazell for commenting on an earlier draft of this essay, and the American Council of Learned Societies for a fellowship that made possible work on the larger project of which this piece forms a part.

1. Frank Norris, *The Octopus: A Story of California* (1901), repr. in *The Complete Edition of Frank Norris,* 10 vols. (Garden City, N.Y.: Doubleday, Doran, & Co., 1928), 2:21. All subsequent references to this work are to this edition, vols. 1 and 2, and are given parenthetically by volume and page number in the text.

2. This move to the Asian marketplace is managed by the industrialist-turned-shipper Cedarquist, who earlier notes that if the "great word" of the nineteenth century was production, "the great word of the twentieth century will be . . . markets" (2:21). The turn to Asia as the new marketplace for American overproduction displays not merely a global and imperialist marketing strategy but also a promotion and exploitation of late nineteenth-century anxieties about masculinity. As the social historian Ronald T. Takaki argues in *Iron Cages: Race and Culture in Nineteenth-Century America* (New York: Alfred A. Knopf, 1979), the imperial outlet for American surplus explicitly was seen as a violent reassertion

of the racial and social "body," as a "masculine thrust toward Asia" (pp. 253–79).

3. On the agrarianist antinomy of producer and speculator, and the economic and aesthetic problems it entails, see Walter Benn Michaels's excellent "Dreiser's *Financier:* The Man of Business as a Man of Letters," in *American Realism: New Essays,* ed. Eric J. Sundquist (Baltimore: Johns Hopkins University Press, 1982), pp. 278–95.

4. Perry Miller, *Life of the Mind in America: From the Revolution to the Civil War* (New York: Harcourt, Brace & World, 1965), p. 293; J. A. Meigs, as quoted by Miller, "The Responsibility of Mind in a Civilization of Machines," *American Scholar* 31 (Winter 1961): 62.

5. Takaki, *Iron Cages,* p. 149.

6. Augustus K. Gardner, *History of the Art of Midwivery* (New York: Stringer & Townshend, 1852), p. 1.

7. G. J. Barker-Benfield, *The Horrors of the Half-Known Life: Male Attitudes toward Women and Sexuality in Nineteenth-Century America* (New York: Harper & Row Publishers, 1976), p. 265.

8. *Animalcule* is a term for microscopic animals but also, and especially before the spermatic function in reproduction was determined (that is, before Oskar Hertwig's account of fertilization in 1876), for spermatozoa. For a brief summary of late nineteenth-century theories of reproduction and fertilization, see Patrick Geddes and J. Arthur Thomson, *The Evolution of Sex* (1889; repr., London and New York: Scribner's, 1899), pp. 156–67.

9. For an informed inventory of naturalist notions of force, see Ronald K. Martin, *American Literature and the Universe of Force* (Durham, N.C.: Duke University Press, 1981); see also William H. Jordy, *Henry Adams: Scientific Historian* (New Haven: Yale University Press, 1952). Harold Kaplan's recent *Power and Order: Henry Adams and the Naturalist Tradition in American Fiction* (Chicago: University of Chicago Press, 1981) tends, like most treatments of American naturalism, to relay rather than examine naturalist "ideologies" of force, taking as its premise a radical antinomy between literary and social forms of power, between art and power, and automatically assuming, for instance, that "even the most sophisticated political theory works at odds with the literary imagination" (p. ix). Important discussions of Norris include: Donald Pizer, *The Novels of Frank Norris* (Bloomington: Indiana University Press, 1966), and the chapters on Norris in Maxwell Geismar, *Rebels and Ancestors: The American Novel, 1890–1915* (Boston: Houghton Mifflin Co., 1953), Kenneth Lynn, *The Dream of Success: A Study of the Modern American*

Imagination (Boston: Little, Brown & Co., 1955), and Larzer Ziff, *The American 1890s: Life and Times of a Lost Generation* (New York: Viking Press, 1966).

10. On the centrality of the thermodynamic model in the nineteenth century, with particular reference to Zola, see Michel Serres's extraordinary *Feux et signaux de brume, Zola* (Paris: Grasset, 1975), and also his *Hermes: Literature, Science, Philosophy,* ed. Josué V. Harari and David F. Bell (Baltimore: Johns Hopkins University Press, 1982).

11. Henry Adams, "A Letter to American Teachers of History," in *The Degradation of the Democratic Dogma* (New York: Macmillan Co., 1920), pp. 144, 140.

12. Thorstein Veblen, *The Theory of the Leisure Class* (1899; repr., New York: New American Library, 1953), pp. 27–28.

13. Ibid., p. 28. Women function as something of a shifter term and even "fall guy" in Veblen's evolutionary theory, representing at once productive industry and the incitement to exploit and waste.

14. Henry Adams, *The Education of Henry Adams* (1918; repr., Boston: Houghton Mifflin Co., 1946), pp. 380, 453, 455–56, 344.

15. Henry Adams, "A Letter to American Teachers of History," p. 231.

16. Henry Adams, *Education of Henry Adams,* p. 387.

17. Theodore Dreiser, *The Financier* (New York: Thomas Y. Crowell Co., 1974), p. 61.

18. I refer here to the notion of "miraculated production" articulated by Gilles Deleuze and Felix Guattari in their discussions of production-machines and of the body as machine in *Anti-Oedipus: Capitalism and Schizophrenia* (Minneapolis: University of Minnesota Press, 1983), esp. ch. 1.

19. Norris's notes and manuscripts are in the Bancroft Library, University of California, Berkeley.

20. Hilma's pregnancy is also juxtaposed, in this scene, to the slaughter of the hyperproductive rabbits; this massacre, in turn, reinvokes the earlier "massacre of innocents" (1:47)—the locomotive's slaughter of the sheep (1:47–48); Annixter, Norris writes, felt "an inane sheepishness when [Hilma] was about" (1:76–77).

21. On the significance of the Medusa figure, see Neil Hertz, "Medusa's Head: Male Hysteria under Political Pressure," *Representations* 4 (Fall 1983): 27–54.

22. Frank Norris, *McTeague,* ed. Donald Pizer (1899; repr. of first ed., New York: W. W. Norton & Co., 1977), p. 213. All subsequent references to this work are to this edition and are cited parenthetically by page number in the text.

23. Rev. John Todd, *The Sunset Land; or, The Great Pacific Slope* (Boston: Lee & Shepard, 1870), pp. 67, 47, 124. Barker-Benfield observes, in *Horrors of the Half-Known Life,* that Todd, among others, viewed "male activities of all kinds, from his own to those of California gold-miners, as the emulation of woman's powers of gestation and parturition" (p. 217).

24. Karl Marx, *Capital* (New York: International Publishers, 1967), 3:827.

25. Frank Norris, *Vandover and the Brute* (1914; repr. of first ed., Lincoln: University of Nebraska Press, 1978), p. 10. All subsequent references to this novel are to this edition and are cited parenthetically by page number in the text.

26. Vandover's art is consistently allied to mechanics; the sites of art in the novel, for instance, are preeminently the Mechanics' Library and the Mechanics' Fair; and Vandover's final artistic work involves the painting of little pictures—of steamships, for example—on the lacquered surfaces of iron safes (p. 314).

27. Joseph Le Conte, "Correlation of Vital with Chemical and Physical Forces," in Balfour Stewart et al., *The Conservation of Energy* (New York: D. Appleton, 1875), pp. 179, 190. Le Conte's naturalist linking of generation and degradation is not at all atypical. See, for instance: Henry Fiske, "The Dependence of Life on Decomposition" (1871), included with the *Pamphlets on Evolution* in the Le Conte collection, Biology Library, University of California, Berkeley.

28. Le Conte, "Correlation of Vital with Chemical and Phyiscal Forces," p. 192.

29. Geddes and Thomson, *Evolution of Sex,* pp. 26, 234. On Geddes, see Jill Conway, "Stereotypes of Femininity in a Theory of Sexual Evolution," in *Suffer and Be Still: Women in the Victorian Age,* ed. Martha Vicinus (Bloomington: Indiana University Press, 1972), pp. 140–54; Philip Boardman, *Patrick Geddes: Maker of the Future* (Chapel Hill: University of North Carolina Press, 1944); and Boardman's *The Worlds of Patrick Geddes* (London: Routledge & Kegan Paul, 1978). It should be noted that the connection between heat and sexual differentiation and reproduction goes back at least to Galen and Aristotle. (See, for instance: Galen, *On the Usefulness of the Parts of the Body,* ed. and trans. Margaret Tallmadge May [Ithaca: Cornell University Press, 1968].) My concern here is with the consequences of the shift from thermic to thermodynamic theories of sexual biology.

30. See my *Henry James and the Art of Power* (Ithaca: Cornell University Press, 1984), esp. the "Postscript," pp. 171–95.

31. Jacques Donzelot, *The Policing of Families,* trans. Robert Hurley (New York: Pantheon Books, 1979), p. 232.

32. Ibid., p. 6. See also: Michel Foucault, "The Subject and Power," *Critical Inquiry* 8 (Summer 1982). The investment in a radical opposition between sexual and economic domains figures prominently even in, or especially in, attempts to locate points of intersection between them—for instance, in attempts to find the missing link between Marxist and feminist analyses. Thus, Catharine A. MacKinnon, in her richly suggestive "Feminism, Marxism, Method, and the State: An Agenda for Theory," in *The Signs Reader: Women, Gender, and Scholarship,* ed. Elizabeth Abel and Emily K. Abel (Chicago: University of Chicago Press, 1983), pp. 227-56, begins by restating such an opposition: "Sexuality is to feminism what work is to marxism: that which is most one's own, yet most taken away." Although this antinomy is insisted upon throughout, MacKinnon further suggests that "instead of engaging the debate over which came (or comes) first, sex or class, the task for theory is to explore the conflicts and connections between the methods that found it meaningful to analyze social conditions in terms of those categories in the first place" (239). I am suggesting that one form such an exploration of conflicts and connections might take is the biopolitical analysis I have outlined here. More locally, MacKinnon is certainly right in stating that a "synthesis" of sexual and economic categories cannot operate simply through an analogizing by which "the marxist meaning of reproduction, the iteration of productive relations, is punned into an analysis of biological reproduction" (238). Rather, what I have tried to focus on here are the naturalist rewritings of production, the ways in which the contradictions and differences between forms of mechanical and biological reproduction become operational.

33. Geddes and Thomson, *Evolution of Sex,* p. 286.

34. Josiah Strong, *The Times and Young Men* (New York, 1901), p. 125.

35. Josiah Strong, *Our Country* (1891; repr., Cambridge, Mass: Harvard University Press, 1963), p. 164.

36. See, for instance: T. J. Jackson Lears, *No Place of Grace: Antimodernism and the Transformation of American Culture, 1880-1920* (New York: Pantheon Books, 1981), and Lears's "From Salvation to Self-Realization: Advertising and the Therapeutic Roots of the Consumer Culture, 1880-1930," in *The Culture of Consumption: Critical Essays in American History, 1880-1980,* ed. Richard Wightman Fox and Lears (New York: Pantheon Books, 1983), pp. 3-38.

37. Michel Foucault, *Discipline and Punish: The Birth of the Prison,* trans. Alan Sheridan (New York: Pantheon Books, 1977), pp. 160-61.

38. For a more detailed treatment of this realist narrative supervision, see my "*The Princess Casamassima:* Realism and the Fantasy of Sur-

veillance," *Nineteenth-Century Fiction* 35 (Mar. 1981): 506–34; repr. in *American Realism: New Essays,* ed. Eric J. Sundquist (Baltimore: Johns Hopkins University Press, 1982), pp. 95–118.

39. Frank Norris, "The Mechanics of Fiction," in *Blix: Moran of the Lady Letty: Essays on Authorship* (New York: P. F. Collier & Son Publishers, 1899), pp. 314, 316; repr. in Norris, *The Responsibilities of the Novelist, Complete Edition* 7:114, 116–17.

Eve Kosofsky Sedgwick

The Beast in the Closet: James and the Writing of Homosexual Panic

I. HISTORICIZING MALE HOMOSEXUAL PANIC

At the age of twenty-five, D. H. Lawrence was excited about the work of James M. Barrie. He felt it helped him understand himself and explain himself. *"Do* read Barrie's *Sentimental Tommy* and *Tommy and Grizel,"* he wrote Jessie Chambers. "They'll help you understand how it is with me. I'm in exactly the same predicament." [1]

Fourteen years later, though, Lawrence placed Barrie among a group of writers whom he considered appropriate objects of authorial violence. "What's the good of being hopeless, so long as one has a hob-nailed boot to kick [them] with? *Down with the Poor in Spirit!* A war! But the Subtlest, most intimate warfare. Smashing the face of what one *knows* is rotten." [2]

It was not only in the intimate warfares of one writer that the years 1910 to 1924 marked changes. But Lawrence's lurch toward a brutal, virilizing disavowal of his early identification with Barrie's sexually irresolute characters reflects two rather different trajectories: first, of course, changes in the historical and intellectual context within which British literature could be read; but second, a hatingly crystallized literalization, as *between* men, of what had been in Barrie's influential novels portrayed as exactly "the Subtlest, most intimate warfare" *within* a man. Barrie's novel sequence was also interested, as Lawrence was not, in the mutilating effects of this masculine civil war on women.

I argue that the Barrie to whom Lawrence reacted with such volatility and finally with such virulence was writing out of a post-Romantic tradition of fictional meditations on the subject specifically of male homosexual panic. The writers whose work I adduce here include—besides Barrie—Thackeray, George Du

Maurier, and James: an odd mix of big and little names. The cheapnesses and compromises of this tradition will, however, turn out to be as important as its freshest angularities, since one of the functions of a tradition *is* to create a path-of-least-resistance (or at the last resort, a pathology-of-least-resistance) for the expression of previously inchoate material.

An additional problem: This tradition was an infusing rather than a generically distinct one in British letters, and it is thus difficult to discriminate it with confidence or to circumscribe it within the larger stream of nineteenth-century fictional writing. But the tradition is worth tracing partly on that very account, as well: the difficult questions of generic and thematic embodiment resonate so piercingly with another set of difficult questions, those precisely of sexual definition and embodiment. The supposed oppositions that characteristically structure this writing—the respectable "versus" the bohemian, the cynical "versus" the sentimental, the provincial "versus" the cosmopolitan, the anesthetized "versus" the sexual—seem to be, among other things, recastings and explorations of another pseudo-opposition that had come by the middle of the nineteenth century to be cripplingly knotted into the guts of British men and, through them, into the lives of women. The name of this pseudo-opposition, when it came to have a name, was homosexual "versus" heterosexual.

Recent sexual historiography by, for instance, Alan Bray in his *Homosexuality in Renaissance England* suggests that until about the time of the Restoration, homophobia in England, while intense, was for the most part highly theologized, was anathematic in tone and structure, and had little cognitive bite as a way for people to perceive and experience their own and their neighbors' actual activities.[3] Homosexuality "was not conceived as part of the created order at all," Bray writes, but as "part of its dissolution. And as such it was not a sexuality in its own right, but existed as a potential for confusion and disorder in one undivided sexuality."[4] If sodomy was the most characteristic expression of anti-nature or the anti-Christ itself, it was nevertheless, or perhaps for that very reason, not an explanation that sprang easily to mind for those sounds from the bed next to one's own—or even for the pleasures of one's own bed. Before the end of the eighteenth century, however, Bray shows, with the beginnings of a crystallized male homosexual role and male homosexual culture, a much sharper-eyed and acutely psychologized secular homophobia was current.

I have argued (in *Between Men: English Literature and Male Homosocial Desire*) that this development was important not only for the persecutory regulation of a nascent minority population of distinctly homosexual men but also for the regulation of the male homosocial bonds that structure *all* culture—at any rate, all public or heterosexual culture.[5] This argument follows Lévi-Strauss in defining culture itself, like marriage, in terms of a "total relationship of exchange . . . not established between a man and a woman, but between two groups of men, [in which] the woman figures only as one of the objects in the exchange, not as one of the partners";[6] or follows Heidi Hartmann in defining patriarchy itself as "*relations between men,* which have a material base, and which, though hierarchical, establish or create interdependence and solidarity among men that enable them to dominate women."[7] To this extent, it makes sense that a newly active concept—a secular, psychologized homophobia—that seemed to offer a new proscriptive or descriptive purchase on the whole continuum of male homosocial bonds, would be a pivotal and embattled concept indeed.

Bray describes the earliest legal persecutions of the post-Restoration gay male subculture, centered in gathering places called "molly houses," as being random and, in his word, "pogrom"-like in structure.[8] I would emphasize the specifically terroristic or exemplary workings of this structure: because a given homosexual man could not know whether or not to expect to be an object of legal violence, the legal enforcement had a disproportionately wide effect. At the same time, however, an opening was made for a subtler strategy in response, a kind of ideological pincers-movement that would extend manyfold the impact of this theatrical enforcement. As *Between Men* argues, under this strategy (or, perhaps better put, in this space of strategic potential),

> not only must homosexual men be unable to ascertain whether they are to be the objects of "random" homophobic violence, but no man must be able to ascertain that he is not (that his bonds are not) homosexual. In this way, a relatively small exertion of physical and legal compulsion potentially rules great reaches of behavior and filiation.
>
> So-called "homosexual panic" is the most private, psychologized form in which many . . . western men experience their vulnerability to the social pressure of homophobic blackmail. [9]

Thus, at least since the eighteenth century in England and America, the continuum of male homosocial bonds has been brutally structured by a secularized and psychologized homophobia, which has excluded certain shiftingly and more or less arbitrarily defined segments of the continuum from participating in the overarching male entitlement—in the complex web of male power over the production, reproduction, and exchange of goods, persons, and meanings. I argue that the historically shifting, and precisely the arbitrary and self-contradictory, nature of the way *homosexuality* (along with its predecessor terms) has been defined in relation to the rest of the male homosocial spectrum has been an exceedingly potent and embattled locus of power over the entire range of male bonds, and perhaps especially over those that define themselves, not *as* homosexual, but *as against* the homosexual. Because the paths of male entitlement, especially in the nineteenth century, required certain intense male bonds that were not readily distinguishable from the most reprobated bonds, an endemic and ineradicable state of what I am calling male homosexual panic became the normal condition of the male heterosexual entitlement.

Some consequences and corollaries of this approach to male relationships should perhaps be made more explicit. To begin with, as I suggested earlier, the approach is not founded on an essential differentiation between "basically homosexual" and "basically heterosexual" men, aside from the historically small group of consciously and self-acceptingly homosexual men, who are no longer susceptible to homosexual panic as I define it here. If such compulsory relationships as male friendship, mentorship, admiring identification, bureaucratic subordination, and heterosexual rivalry all involve forms of investment that force men into the arbitrarily mapped, self-contradictory, and anathema-riddled quicksands of the middle distance of male homosocial desire, then it appears that men enter into adult masculine entitlement only through acceding to the permanent threat that the small space they have cleared for themselves on this terrain may always, just as arbitrarily and with just as much justification, be punitively and retroactively foreclosed.

The result of men's accession to this double bind is, first, the acute *manipulability,* through the fear of one's own "homosexuality," of acculturated men; and second, a reservoir of potential for *violence* caused by the self-ignorance that this regime constitutively enforces. The historical emphasis on homophobic enforcement in the armed services in, for instance, England and the United States supports this analysis. In these institutions, where both men's manipulability and their potential for violence are at the highest possible premium, the *pre*scription of the most intimate male bonding and the *pro*scription of (the remarkably cognate) "homosexuality" are both stronger than in civilian society—are, in fact, close to absolute.

My specification of widespread, endemic male homosexual panic as a post-Romantic phenomenon rather than as coeval with the beginnings, under homophobic pressure, of a distinctive male homosexual culture a century or so earlier, has to do with (what I read as) the centrality of the paranoid Gothic[10] as the literary genre in which homophobia found its most apt and ramified embodiment. Homophobia found in the paranoid Gothic a genre of its own, not because the genre provided a

platform for expounding an already-formed homophobic ideology—of course, it did no such thing—but through a more active,
polylogic engagement of "private" with "public" discourses, as
in the wildly dichotomous play around solipsism and intersubjectivity of a male paranoid plot like that of *Frankenstein*. The
transmutability of the intrapsychic with the intersubjective in
these plots where one man's mind could be read by that of the
feared and desired other; the urgency and violence with which
these plots reformed large, straggly, economically miscellaneous
families such as the Frankensteins in the ideologically hyposta-
tized image of the tight Oedipal family; and then the extra
efflorescence of violence with which the remaining female term
in these triangular families was elided, leaving, as in *Frankenstein,*
a residue of two potent male figures locked in an epistemologi-
cally indissoluble clench of will and desire—through these means,
the paranoid Gothic powerfully signified, at the very moment
of crystallization of the modern, capitalism-marked Oedipal
family, the inextricability from that formation of a strangling
double bind in male homosocial constitution. Put another way,
the usefulness of Freud's formulation, in the case of Dr. Schreber,
that paranoia in men results from the repression of their homosexual desire,[11] has nothing to do with a classification of the
paranoid Gothic in terms of "latent" or "overt" "homosexual"
"types," but everything to do with the foregrounding, under
the specific, foundational historic conditions of the early Gothic,
of intense male homosocial desire as at once the most compulsory and the most prohibited of social bonds.

To inscribe that vulgar classification supposedly derived from
Freud on what was arguably the founding moment of the world
view and social constitution that he codified would hardly be
enlightening. Still, the newly formulated and stressed "universal"
imperative/prohibition attached to male homosocial desire, even
given that its claim for universality already excluded (the female)
half of the population, nevertheless required, of course, further
embodiment and specification in new taxonomies of personality

and character. These taxonomies would mediate between the supposedly classless, "personal" entities of the ideological fictions and the particular, class-specified, economically inscribed lives that they influenced; and at the same time, the plethoric and apparently comprehensive pluralism of the taxonomies occluded, through the illusion of choice, the overarching existence of the double bind that structured them all.

Recent gay male historiography, influenced by Foucault, has been especially good at unpacking and interpreting those parts of the nineteenth-century systems of classification that clustered most closely around what current taxonomies construe as "the homosexual." The "sodomite," the "invert," the "homosexual," the "heterosexual" himself, all are objects of historically and institutionally explicable construction.[12] In the discussion of male homosexual *panic,* however—the treacherous middle stretch of the modern homosocial continuum, and the terrain from whose wasting rigors *only* the homosexual-identified man is at all exempt—a different and less distinctly sexualized range of categories needs to be opened up. Again, however, it bears repeating that the object of doing that is not to arrive at a more accurate or up-to-date assignment of "diagnostic" categories, but to better understand the broad field of forces within which masculinity—and thus, *at least* for men, humanity itself—could (can) at a particular moment construct itself.

I want to suggest here that with Thackeray and other early and mid-Victorians, a character classification of "the bachelor" came into currency, a type that for some men both narrowed the venue, and at the same time startlingly desexualized the question, of male sexual choice.[13] Later in the century, when a medical and social-science model of "the homosexual man" had institutionalized this classification for a few men, the broader issue of endemic male homosexual panic was again up for grabs in a way that was newly redetached from character taxonomy and was more apt to be described narratively, as a decisive moment of choice in the developmental labyrinth of the generic individual (male). As the unmarried gothic hero had once been, the bachelor became once again the representative man: James wrote in his 1881 *Notebook*, "I take [London] as an artist and as a bachelor; as one who has the passion of observation and whose business is the study of human life."[14] In the work of writers like Du Maurier, Barrie, and James, among others, male homosexual panic was acted out as a sometimes agonized sexual anesthesia that was damaging to both its male subjects and its female nonobjects. The paranoid Gothic itself, a generic structure that seemed to have been domesticated in the development of the bachelor taxonomy, returned in some of these works as a formally intrusive and incongruous, but strikingly persistent, literary element.[15]

II. MEET MR. BATCHELOR

"Batchelor, my elderly Tiresias,
are you turned into a lovely young
lady par hasard?"
        "Get along, you absurd Trump-
erian professor!" say I.
                                    —*Thackeray*[16]

In Victorian fiction, it is perhaps the figure of the urban bachelor, especially as popularized by Thackeray, who personifies the most deflationary tonal contrast to the eschatological harrowings and epistemological doublings of the paranoid Gothic. Where the Gothic hero had been solipsistic, the bachelor hero is selfish. Where the Gothic hero had raged, the bachelor hero bitches. Where the Gothic hero had been suicidally inclined, the bachelor hero is a hypochondriac. The Gothic hero ranges from euphoria to despondency—the bachelor hero, from the eupeptic to the dyspeptic.

Structurally, moreover, whereas the Gothic hero had personified the concerns and tones of an entire genre, the bachelor is a distinctly circumscribed and often a marginalized figure in the books he inhabits. Sometimes, like Archie Clavering, Major Pendennis, and Jos Sedley, he is simply a minor character; but even when he is putatively the main character, like Surtees's hero "Soapey" Sponge, he more often functions as a clotheshorse or comic place-marker in a discursive plot.[17] The bachelor hero can only be mock-heroic: not merely diminished and parodic himself, he symbolizes the diminution and undermining of certain heroic and totalizing possibilities of generic embodiment. The novel of which the absurd Jos Sedley is not the hero is a novel *without* a hero.

It makes sense, I think, to see the development of this odd character the bachelor, and his dissolutive relation to romantic genre, as, among other things, a move toward the recuperation as character taxonomy of the endemic double bind of male homosexual panic that had been acted out in the paranoid Gothic as plot and structure. This recuperation is perhaps best described as, in several senses, a domestication. Most obviously, in the increasingly stressed nineteenth-century bourgeois dichotomy between domestic female space and extrafamilial, political and economic male space, the bachelor is at least partly feminized by his attention to and interest in domestic concerns. (At the same time, though, his intimacy with clubland and bohemia gives him a special passport to the world of men, as well.) Then, too, the disruptive and self-ignorant potential for violence in the Gothic hero is replaced in the bachelor hero by physical timidity and, often, by a high valuation on introspection and by (at least partial) self-knowledge. Finally, the bachelor is housebroken by the severing of his connections with a discourse of genital sexuality.

The first-person narrators of much of Thackeray's later fiction are good examples of the urban bachelor in his major key. Even though the Pendennis who narrates *The Newcomes* and *Philip* is supposedly married, his voice, personality, and tastes are strikingly similar to those of the archetypal Thackeray bach-

elor, the narrator of his novella *Lovel the Widower* (1859)—a
man called, by no coincidence at all, Mr. Batchelor. (Of course,
Thackeray's own ambiguous marital status—married, but to an
inveterately sanitarium-bound, psychotically depressed woman—
facilitated this slippage in the narrators whom Thackeray seemed
to model on himself.) Mr. Batchelor is, as James says of Olive
Chancellor, unmarried by every implication of his being. He is
compulsively garrulous about marital prospects, his own (past
and present) among others, but always in a tone that points, in
one way or another, to the absurdity of the thought. For instance, his hyperbolic treatment of an early romantic disappointment is used both to mock and undermine the importance to
him of that incident, and at the same time, by invidious com-
parison, to discredit in advance the seriousness of any later
involvement:

> Some people have the small-pox twice; *I do not.* In my case, if a heart
> is broke, it's broke: if a flower is withered, it's withered. If I choose to
> put my grief in a ridiculous light, why not? why do you suppose I am
> going to make a tragedy of such an old, used-up, battered, stale, vulgar,
> trivial every-day subject as a jilt who plays with a man's passion, and
> laughs at him, and leaves him? Tragedy indeed! Oh, yes! poison—black-
> edged note-paper—Waterloo Bridge—one more unfortunate, and so
> forth! No: if she goes, let her go! —*si celeres quatit pennas,* I puff the
> what-d'ye-call-it away! (Ch. 2)

The plot of *Lovel*—slight enough—is an odd local station on the
subway from *Liber Amoris* to Proust. Mr. Batchelor, when he
lived in lodgings, had had a slightly tender friendship with his
landlady's daughter Bessy, who at that time helped support her
family by dancing in a music hall. A few years later, he gets her
installed as governess in the home of his friend Lovel, the widower. Several men in the vicinity are rivals for Bessy's affections:
the local doctor, the shrewd autodidact butler, and, halfhearted-
ly, Batchelor himself. When a visiting bounder attacks Bessy's
reputation and her person, Batchelor, who is eavesdropping on
the scene, fatally hesitates in coming to her defense, suddenly

full of doubts about her sexual purity ("Fiends and anguish! he had known her before" [Ch. 5]) and his own eagerness for marriage. Finally it is the autodidact butler who rescues her, and Lovel himself who marries her.

If the treatment of the romantic possibilities that are supposedly at the heart of *Lovel* has a tendency to dematerialize them almost before they present themselves, the treatment of certain other physical pleasures is given an immediacy that seems correspondingly heightened. In fact, the substantiality of physical pleasure is explicitly linked to the state of bachelorhood.

> To lie on that comfortable, cool bachelor's bed. . . . Once at Shrublands I heard steps pacing overhead at night, and the feeble but continued wail of an infant. I wakened from my sleep, was sulky, but turned and slept again. Biddlecombe the barrister I knew was the occupant of the upper chamber. He came down the next morning looking wretchedly yellow about the cheeks, and livid round the eyes. His teething infant had kept him on the march all night. . . . He munched a shred of toast, and was off by the omnibus to chambers. I chipped a second egg; I may have tried one or two other nice little things on the table (Strasbourg pâté I know I never can resist, and am convinced it is perfectly wholesome). I could see my own sweet face in the mirror opposite, and my gills were as rosy as any broiled salmon. (Ch. 3)

Unlike its sacramental, community-building function in Dickens, food in Thackeray—even good food—is most apt to signify the bitterness of dependency or inequality. The exchange value of food and drink, its expensiveness or cheapness relative to the status and expectations of those who partake, the ostentation or stinginess with which it is doled out, or the meanness with which it is cadged, mark out for it a shifty and invidious path through each of Thackeray's books, including this one. The rounded Pickwickian self-complacency of the rosy-gilled bachelor at breakfast is, then, all the more striking by contrast. In Thackeray's bitchy art where, as in James's, the volatility of the perspective regularly corrodes both the object and the subject of perception, there are moments when the bachelor hero, exactly through his celibacy and selfishness, can seem the only human particle atomized enough to plump through unscathed.

Sometimes unscathed; never unscathing. Of course one of the main pleasures of reading this part of Thackeray's oeuvre is precisely its feline gratuitousness of aggression. At odd moments we are apt to find kitty's unsheathed claws a millimeter from our own eyes. "Nothing, dear friend, escapes your penetration: if a joke is made in your company, you are down upon it instanter, and your smile rewards the wag who amuses you: so you knew at once. . . ." (Ch. 1). When one bachelor consults another bachelor about a third bachelor, nothing is left but ears and whiskers.

> During my visit to London, I had chanced to meet my friend Captain Fitzb—dle, who belongs to a dozen clubs, and knows something of every man in London. "Know anything of Clarence Baker?" "Of course I do," says Fitz; "and if you want any *renseignement,* my dear fellow, I have the honor to inform you that a blacker little sheep does not trot the London *pavé* . . . . know anything of Clarence Baker! My dear fellow, enough to make your hair turn white, unless (as I sometimes fondly imagine) nature has already performed that process, when of course I can't pretend to act upon mere hair-dye." (The whiskers of the individual who addressed me, innocent, stared me in the face as he spoke, and were dyed of the most unblushing purple.) . . . ". . . . From the garrison towns where he has been quartered, he has carried away not only the hearts of the milliners, but their gloves, haberdashery, and perfumery." (Ch. 4)

If, as I am suggesting, Thackeray's bachelors created or reinscribed as a personality type one possible path of response to the strangulation of homosexual panic, their basic strategy is easy enough to trace: a preference of atomized male individualism to the nuclear family (and a corresponding demonization of women, especially of mothers); a garrulous and visible refusal of anything that could be interpreted as genital sexuality, toward objects male or female; a corresponding emphasis on the pleasures of the other senses; and a well-defended social facility that

freights with a good deal of magnetism its proneness to parody
and to unpredictable sadism.

I must say that this does not strike me as a portrait of an exclusively Victorian human type. To refuse sexual choice, in a
society where sexual choice for men is both compulsory and
always self-contradictory, seems, at least for educated men, still
often to involve invoking the precedent of this nineteenth-century persona—not Mr. Batchelor himself perhaps, but generically,
the self-centered and at the same time self-marginalizing bachelor
he represents. Nevertheless, this persona *is* highly specified as a
figure of the nineteenth-century metropolis. He has close ties
with the *flâneurs* of Poe, Baudelaire, Wilde, Benjamin. What is
most importantly specified is his pivotal class position between
the respectable bourgeoisie and bohemia—a bohemia that, again,
Thackeray in the Pendennis novels half invented for English
literature and half merely housetrained.

Literally, it was Thackeray who introduced both the word
and the concept of bohemia to England from Paris.[18] As a sort
of reserve labor force and a semiporous, liminal space for voca-
tional sorting and social rising and falling, bohemia could seemingly be entered from any social level; but, at least in these
literary versions, it served best the cultural needs, the fantasy
needs, and the needs for positive and negative self-definition of
an anxious and conflicted bourgeoisie. Except to homosexual
men, the idea of "bohemia" seems before the 1890s not to have
had a distinctively gay coloration. In these bachelor novels the
simple absence of an enforcing family structure was allowed to
perform its enchantment in a more generalized way; and the most
passionate male comradeship subsisted in an apparently loose relation to the erotic uses of a common pool of women. It might be
more accurate, however, to see the flux of bohemia as the *temporal* space where the young, male bourgeois literary subject was
required to navigate his way through his "homosexual panic"—
seen here as a *developmental* stage—toward the more repressive,

self-ignorant, and apparently consolidated status of the mature bourgeois *paterfamilias.*

Among Thackeray's progeny in the exploration of bourgeois bachelors in bohemia, the most self-conscious and important are Du Maurier, Barrie, and—in a book like *The Ambassadors*—James. The filiations of this tradition are multiple and heterogeneous. For instance, Du Maurier offered James the plot of *Trilby* years before he wrote the novel himself.[19] Or again, Little Bilham in *The Ambassadors* seems closely related to Little Billee, the hero of *Trilby,* a small girlish-looking Left Bank art student. Little Billee shares a studio with two older, bigger, more virile English artists, whom he loves deeply—a bond that seems to give erotic point to Du Maurier's use of the Thackeray naval ballad from which Du Maurier, in turn, had taken Little Billee's name.

> There was gorging Jack and guzzling Jimmy,
> And the youngest he was little Billee.
> Now when they got as far as the Equator
> They's nothing left but one split pea.
>
> Says gorging Jack to guzzling Jimmy,
> "I am extremely hungaree."
> To gorging Jack says guzzling Jimmy,
> "We've nothing left, us must eat we."
>
> Says gorging Jack to guzzling Jimmy,
> "With one another we shouldn't agree!
> There's little Bill, he's young and tender,
> We're old and tough, so let's eat he.
>
> "Oh! Billy, we're going to kill and eat you,
> So undo the button of your chemie. . . ."[20]

As one moves past Thackeray toward the turn of the century, toward the ever greater visibility across class lines of a medicalized discourse of—and newly punitive assaults on—male homosexuality, however, the comfortably frigid campiness of Thackeray's bachelors gives way to something that sounds more inescapably like panic. Mr. Batchelor had played at falling in love with women, but felt no urgency about proving that he actually could. For the bachelor heroes of *Trilby* and *Tommy and Grizel,* though, even that renunciatory high ground of male sexlessness has been strewn with psychic landmines.

In fact, the most consistent keynote of this late literature is exactly the explicitly thematized sexual anesthesia of its heroes. In each of these fictions, moreover, the hero's agonistic and denied sexual anesthesia is treated as being *at the same time* an aspect of a particular, idiosyncratic personality type *and also* an expression of a great Universal. Little Billee, for instance, the hero of *Trilby,* attributes his sudden inability to desire a woman to "a pimple" inside his "bump of" "fondness"—"for that's what's the matter with me—a pimple—just a little clot of blood at the root of a nerve, and no bigger than a pin's point!"[21] In the same long monologue, however, he again attributes his lack of desire, not to the pimple, but on a far different scale to his status as Post-Darwinian Man, unable any longer to believe in God. "Sentimental" Tommy, similarly, the hero of Barrie's eponymous novel and also of *Tommy and Grizel,* is treated throughout each of these astonishingly acute and self-hating novels both as a man with a crippling moral and psychological defect and as the very type of the great creative artist.

III. READING JAMES STRAIGHT

James's "The Beast in the Jungle" (1902) is one of the bachelor fictions of this period that seems to make a strong implicit claim of "universal" applicability through heterosexual symmetries, but that is most movingly subject to a change of Gestalt and of visible saliencies as soon as an assumed heterosexual male norm is at all interrogated. Like *Tommy and Grizel,* the story is of a man and a woman who have a decades-long intimacy. In both stories, the woman desires the man but the man fails to desire the woman. In fact—in each story—the man simply fails to desire at all. Sentimental Tommy desperately desires to feel desire; confusingly counterfeits a desire for Grizel; and, with all the best intentions, finally drives her mad. John Marcher, in James's story, does not even know that desire is absent from his life, nor that May Bartram desires him, until after she has died from his obtuseness.

To judge from the biographies of Barrie and James, each author seems to have made erotic choices that were complicated enough, shifting enough in the gender of their objects, and, at least for long periods, kept distant enough from *éclaircissement* or physical expression, to make each an emboldening figure for a literary discussion of male homosexual panic.[22] Barrie had an almost unconsummated marriage, an unconsummated passion for a married woman (George Du Maurier's daughter!), and a lifelong uncategorizable passion for her family of sons. James had—well, exactly that which we now all know that we know not. Oddly, however, it is simpler to read the psychological plot of *Tommy and Grizel*—the horribly thorough and conscientious ravages on a woman of a man's compulsion to pretend he desires her—into the cryptic and tragic story of James's involvement with Constance Fenimore Woolson, than to read it directly into any incident of Barrie's life. It is hard to read Leon Edel's account of James's sustained (or repeated) and intense, but peculiarly furtive,[23] intimacies with this deaf, intelligent American woman author who clearly loved him, without coming to a grinding sense that James felt he had with her above all something, sexually, to prove. And it is hard to read about what seems to have been her suicide without wondering whether the expense of James's heterosexual self-probation—an expense, one envisions if one has Barrie in mind, of sudden "generous" "yielding" impulses in him and equally sudden revulsions—was not charged most intimately to this secreted-away companion of so many of his travels and residencies. If this is true, the working-out of his denied homosexual panic must have been only the more grueling for the woman in proportion to James's outrageous gift and his moral magnetism.

If something like the doubly destructive interaction I am sketching here did in fact occur between James and Constance Fenimore Woolson, then its structure has been resolutely reproduced by virtually all the critical discussion of James's writing. James's mistake here, biographically, seems to have been in moving blindly from a sense of the good, the desirability, of love and sexuality, to the automatic imposition on himself of a specifically *hetero*sexual compulsion. (I say "imposition on himself," but of course he did not invent the heterosexual specificity of this compulsion—he merely failed, at this point in his life, to resist it actively.) The easy assumption (by James, the society, and the critics) that sexuality and heterosexuality are always exactly translatable into one another is, obviously, homophobic. Importantly, too, it is deeply heterophobic: it denies the very possibility of *difference* in desires, in objects. One is no longer surprised, of course, at the repressive blankness on these issues of most literary criticism; but for James, in whose life the pattern of homosexual desire was brave enough and resilient enough to be at last biographically inobliterable, one might have hoped that in criticism of his work the possible differences of different erotic paths would not be so ravenously subsumed under a compulsorily—and hence, never a truly "hetero"— heterosexual model. With strikingly few exceptions, however, the criticism has actively repelled any inquiry into the asymmetries of gendered desire.

It is possible that critics have been motivated in this active incuriosity by a desire to protect James from homophobic misreadings in a perennially repressive sexual climate. It is possible that they fear that, because of the asymmetrically marked structure of heterosexual discourse, *any* discussion of homosexual desires or literary content will marginalize him (or them?) as, simply, *homosexual.* It is possible that they desire to protect him from what they imagine as anachronistically "gay" readings, based on a late twentieth-century vision of men's desire for men that is more stabilized and culturally compact than James's own. It is possible that they read James himself as, in his work, positively refusing or evaporating this element of his eros, translating lived homosexual desires, where he had them, into written heterosexual ones so thoroughly and so successfully that the difference *makes* no difference, the transmutation leaves no residue. Or it is possible that, believing—as I do—that James often, though not always, attempted such a disguise or transmutation, but reliably left a residue both of material that he did not attempt to transmute and of material that could be transmuted only rather violently and messily, some critics are reluctant to undertake the "attack" on James's candor or artistic unity that could be the next step of that argument. Any of these critical motives would be understandable, but their net effect is the usual repressive one of elision and subsumption of supposedly embarrassing material. In dealing with the multiple valences of sexuality, critics' choices should not be limited to crudities of disruption or silences of orthodox enforcement.

Even Leon Edel, who traced out *both* James's history with Constance Fenimore Woolson *and* some of the narrative of his erotic desires for men, connects "The Beast in the Jungle" to the history of Woolson,[24] but connects neither of these to the specificity of James's—or of any—sexuality. The result of this hammeringly tendentious blur in virtually all the James criticism is, for the interpretation of "The Beast in the Jungle," seemingly in the interests of showing it as universally applicable (e.g., about "the artist"), to assume without any space for doubt that the moral point of the story is not only that May Bartram desired John Marcher but that John Marcher *should have desired* May Bartram.

Tommy and Grizel is clearer-sighted on what is essentially the same point. "*Should have desired,*" that novel graphically shows, not only is nonsensical as a moral judgment but is the very mechanism that enforces and perpetuates the mutilating charade of heterosexual exploitation. (James's compulsive use of Woolson, for instance.) Grizel's tragedy is not that the man she desires fails to desire her—which would be sad, but, the book makes clear, endurable—but that he pretends to desire her, and intermittently even convinces himself that he desires her, when he does not.

Impressively, too, the clarity with which *Tommy and Grizel* conveys this process and its ravages seems *not* to be dependent on a given, naive, or monolithic idea of what it would mean for a man to "really" desire someone. On that issue the novel seems to remain agnostic—leaving open the possibility that there is some rather different quantity that is "real" male desire, or alternatively that it is only more and less intermittent infestations of the same murderous syndrome that fuel any male eros at all. That the worst violence of heterosexuality comes with the male *compulsion to desire* women and its attendant deceptions of self and other, however, Barrie says quite decisively.

Tommy and Grizel is an extraordinary, and an unjustly forgotten, novel. What has dated it and keeps it from being a great novel, in spite of the acuteness with which it treats male desire, is the—one can hardly help saying Victorian—mawkish opportunism with which it figures the desire of women. Permissibly, the novel's real imaginative and psychological energies focus entirely on the hero. Impermissibly—and here the structure of the novel itself exactly reproduces the depredations of its hero— there is a moralized pretense at an equal focus on a rounded, autonomous, imaginatively and psychologically invested female protagonist, who however—far from being novelistically "desired" in herself—is really, transparently, created in the precise negative image of the hero, created to be the single creature in the world who is most perfectly fashioned to be caused the most exquisite pain and intimate destruction by him and him only. The fit is excruciatingly seamless. Grizel is the daughter of a mad prostitute, whose legacies to her—aside from vitality, intelligence, imagination—have been a strong sensuality and a terror (which the novel highly valorizes) of having that sensuality stirred. It was acute of Barrie to see that this is the exact woman—were such a woman possible—who, appearing strong and autonomous, would be most unresistingly annihilable precisely by Tommy's two-phase rhythm of sexual come-on followed by repressive frigidity, and his emotional geology of pliant sweetness fundamented by unyielding compulsion. But the prurient exactitude of the female fit, as of a creature bred for sexual sacrifice without resistance or leftovers, drains the authority of the novel to make an uncomplicit judgment on Tommy's representative value.

Read in this context, "The Beast in the Jungle" looks—from the point of view of female desire—potentially revolutionary. Whoever May Bartram is and whatever she wants (I discuss this more later), clearly at least the story has the Jamesian negative virtue of not pretending to present her rounded and whole. She is an imposing character, but—*and*—a bracketed one. James's bravura in manipulating point of view lets him dissociate himself critically from John Marcher's selfishness—from the sense that there is no *possibility* of a subjectivity other than Marcher's own—but lets him leave himself in place of that selfishness finally an *askesis,* a particular humility of point of view as being *limited* to Marcher's. Of May Bartram's history, of her emotional determinants, of her erotic structures, the reader learns very little; we are permitted, if we pay attention at all, to *know* that we have learned very little. Just as, in Proust, it is always open to any minor or grotesque character to turn out at any time to have a major artistic talent with which, however, the novel does not happen to busy itself, so "The Beast in the Jungle" seems to give the reader permission to imagine some female needs and desires and gratifications that are not structured exactly in the image of Marcher's or of the story's own laws.

It is only the last scene of the story—Marcher's last visit to May Bartram's grave—that conceals or denies the humility, the incompleteness of the story's presentation of her subjectivity. This is the scene in which Marcher's sudden realization that *she* has felt and expressed desire for *him* is, as it seems, answered in an intensely symmetrical, "conclusive" rhetorical clinch by the narrative/authorial prescription: "The escape would have been to love her; then, *then* he would have lived."[25] The paragraph that follows, the last in the story, has the same climactic, authoritative (even authoritarian) rhythm of supplying Answers in the form of symmetrical supplementarities. For this single, this conclusive, this formally privileged moment in the story—this resolution over the dead body of May Bartram—James and Marcher are presented as coming together, Marcher's revelation underwritten by James's rhetorical authority, and James's epistemological askesis gorged, for once, beyond recognition, by Marcher's compulsive, ego-projective certainties. In the absence of May Bartram, the two men, author/narrator and hero, are reunited at last in the confident, shared, masculine knowledge of what she Really Wanted and what she Really Needed. And what she Really Wanted and Really Needed show, of course, an uncanny closeness to what Marcher Really (should have) Wanted and Needed, himself.

Imagine "The Beast in the Jungle" without this enforcing symmetry. Imagine (remember) the story with May Bartram alive.[26] Imagine a possible alterity. And the name of alterity is not *always* "woman." What if Marcher himself had other desires?

IV. THE LAW OF THE JUNGLE

Names . . . *Assingham—Padwick—*
Lutch—Marfle—Bross—Crapp—
*Didcock—Wichells—*Putchin*—Brind—*
Coxeter—Coxster . . . Dickwinter
. . . *Jakes . . . Marcher—*
        —*(James,* Notebook, *1901)*

There has so far seemed no reason, or little reason, why what I have been calling "male homosexual panic" could not just as descriptively have been called "male heterosexual panic"—or, simply, "male sexual panic." Although I began with a structural and historicizing narrative that emphasized the pre- and proscriptively defining importance of men's bonds with men, potentially including genital bonds, the books I have discussed have not, for the most part, seemed to center emotionally or thematically on such bonds. In fact, it is, explicitly, a male panic in the face of *hetero*sexuality that many of these books most describe. It is all very well to insist, as I have done, that homosexual panic is necessarily a problem only, but endemically, of nonhomosexual-identified men; nevertheless the lack in these books of an embodied male-homosexual thematics, however inevitable, has had a dissolutive effect on the structure and texture of such an argument. Part, although only part, of the reason for that lack was historical: it was only close to the end of the nineteenth century that a cross-class homosexual role and a consistent, ideologically full thematic discourse of male homosexuality became entirely visible, in developments that were publicly dramatized in—though far from confined to—the Wilde trials.

In "The Beast in the Jungle," written at the threshold of the new century, the possibility of an embodied male-homosexual thematics has, I would like to argue, a precisely liminal presence. It is present as a—as a very particular, historicized—thematics of absence, and specifically of the absence of speech. The first (in some ways the only) thing we learn about John Marcher is that he has a "secret" (358), a destiny, a something unknown in his future. "You said," May Bartram reminds him, "you had from your earliest time, as the deepest thing within you, the sense of being kept for something rare and strange, possibly prodigious and terrible, that was sooner or later to happen" (359). I would argue that to the extent that Marcher's secret has *a* content, that content is homosexual.

Of course the extent to which Marcher's secret has anything

that could be called a content is, not only dubious, but in the
climactic last scene actively denied. "He had been the man of his
time, *the* man, to whom nothing on earth was to have happened"
(401). The denial that the secret has a content—the assertion
that its content is precisely a lack—is a stylish and "satisfyingly"
Jamesian formal gesture. The apparent gap of meaning that it
points to is, however, far from being a genuinely empty one; it
is no sooner asserted than filled to a plenitude with the most
orthodox of ethical enforcements. To point rhetorically to the
emptiness of the secret, "the nothing that is," is, in fact, oddly,
the same gesture as the attribution to it of a compulsory content about heterosexuality—of the content specifically, "He
should [have] desire[d] her."

> *She* was what he had missed. . . . The fate he had been marked for he
> had met with a vengeance—he had emptied the cup to the lees; he had
> been the man of his time, *the* man, to whom nothing on earth was to
> have happened. That was the rare stroke—that was his visitation. . . .
> This the companion of his vigil had at a given moment made out, and
> she had then offered him the chance to baffle his doom. One's doom,
> however, was never baffled, and on the day she told him his own had
> come down she had seen him but stupidly stare at the escape she
> offered him.
>
> The escape would have been to love her; then, *then* he would have
> lived. (401)

The "empty" meaning of Marcher's unspeakable doom is
thus necessarily, specifically heterosexual; it refers to the perfectly specific absence of a prescribed heterosexual desire. If
critics, eager to help James moralize this ending, persist in claim-
ing to be able to translate freely and without residue from that
(absent) heterosexual desire to an abstraction of all possibilities
of human love, there are, I think, good reasons for trying to
slow them down. The totalizing, insidiously symmetrical view
that the "nothing" that is Marcher's unspeakable fate is necessarily a mirror image of the "everything" he could and should

have had is, specifically, in an *oblique* relation to a very different
history of meanings for assertions of the erotic negative.

The "full" meaning of that unspeakable fate, on the other
hand, comes from the centuries-long historical chain of substantive uses of space-clearing negatives to void and at the same time
to underline the possibility of male homosexual genitality. The
rhetorical name for this figure is *preterition.* Unspeakable, Un-
mentionable, *nefandam libidinem,* "that sin which should be
neither named nor committed,"[27] the "detestable and abominable sin, amongst Christians not to be named,"

> Whose vice in special, if I would declare,
> It were enough for to perturb the air,

"things fearful to name," "the obscene sound of the unbeseem-
ing words,"

> A sin so odious that the fame of it
> Will fright the damned in the darksome pit,[28]

"the Love that dare not speak its name,"[29]—such *were* the speak-
able nonmedical terms, in Christian tradition, of the homosexual
possibility for men. The marginality of these terms' semantic
and ontological status as substantive nouns reflected and shaped
the exiguousness—but also, the potentially enabling secrecy—of
that "possibility." And the newly specifying, reifying medical
and penal public discourse of the male homosexual role, in the
years around the Wilde trials, far from retiring or obsolescing
these preteritive names, seems instead to have packed them more
firmly and distinctively with homosexual meaning.[30]

John Marcher's "secret" (358), "his singularity" (366), "the
thing she knew, which grew to be at last, with the consecration
of the years, never mentioned between them save as 'the real
truth' about him" (366), "the abyss" (375), "his queer consciousness" (378), "the great vagueness" (379), "the secret of
the gods" (379), "what ignominy or what monstrosity" (379),

"dreadful things . . . I couldn't name" (381): the ways in which the story refers to Marcher's secret fate have the same quasi-nominative, quasi-obliterative structure.

There are, as well, some "fuller," though still highly equivocal, lexical pointers to a homosexual meaning: "The rest of the world of course thought him *queer,* but she, she only, knew how, and above all why, queer; which was precisely what enabled her to dispose the concealing veil in the right folds. She took his *gaiety* from him—since it had to pass with them for gaiety—as she took everything else. . . . She traced his unhappy *perversion* through reaches of its course into which he could scarce follow it" (367; emphasis added). Still, it is mostly in the reifying grammar of periphrasis and preterition—"such a cataclysm" (360), "the great affair" (360), "the catastrophe" (361), "his predicament" (364), "their real truth" (368), "his inevitable topic" (371), "all that they had thought, first and last" (372), "horrors" (382), something "more monstrous than all the monstrosities we've named" (383), "all the loss and all the shame that are thinkable" (384)—that a homosexual meaning becomes, to the degree that it does become, legible. "I don't focus it. I can't name it. I only know I'm exposed" (372).

I am convinced, however, that part of the point of the story is that the reifying effect of periphrasis and preterition on this particular meaning is, if anything, *more* damaging than (though not separable from) its obliterative effect. To have succeeded— which was not to be taken for granted—in cracking the centuries-old code by which the-articulated-denial-of-articulability always had the possibility of meaning two things, of meaning either (heterosexual) "nothing" or "homosexual meaning," would also always have been to assume one's place in a discourse in which there was *a* homosexual meaning, in which all homosexual meaning meant a single thing. To crack a code and enjoy the reassuring exhilarations of knowingness is to buy into the specific formula, "We Know What That Means." (I assume it is this mechanism that makes even critics who know about the male-erotic pathways of James's personal desires appear to be so untroubled about leaving them out of accounts of his writing.[31] As if this form of desire were the most calculable, the simplest to add or subtract or allow for in moving between life and art!) But if, as I suggested in Section I, men's accession to heterosexual entitlement has, for these modern centuries, always been on the ground of a cultivated and compulsory denial of the *un*knowability, of the arbitrariness and self-contradictoriness, of homosexual/heterosexual definition, then the fearful or triumphant interpretive formula "We Know What That Means" seems to take on an odd centrality. First, it is a lie. But second, it is the particular lie that animates and perpetuates the mechanism of homophobic male self-ignorance and violence and manipulability.

It is worth, then, trying to discriminate the possible plurality of meanings behind the unspeakables of "The Beast in the Jungle." To point, as I argue that the narrative itself points and as we have so far pointed, simply to *a* possibility of "homosexual meaning," is to say worse than nothing—it is to pretend to say one thing. But even on the surface of the story, the secret, "*the* thing," "the thing she knew," is discriminated, first of all discriminated temporally. There are at least two secrets: Marcher feels that he knows, but has never told anyone but May Bartram (secret number one) that he is reserved for some very particular, uniquely rending fate in the future, whose nature is (secret number two) unknown to himself. Over the temporal extent of the story, both the balance, between the two characters, of cognitive mastery over the secrets' meanings, and the temporal placement, between future and past, of the second secret, shift; it is possible, in addition, that the actual content (if any) of the secrets changes with these temporal and cognitive changes, if time and intersubjectivity are of the essence of the secrets.

Let me baldly, then, spell out my hypothesis of what a series of "full"—that is, homosexually tinged—meanings for the Unspeakable might look like for this story, differing both over time and according to character.

For John Marcher, let us hypothesize, the future secret—the secret of his hidden fate—importantly includes, though it is not necessarily limited to, the possibility of something homosexual. *For Marcher,* the presence or possibility of a homosexual meaning attached to the inner, the future secret, has exactly the reifying, totalizing, and blinding effect we described earlier in regard to the phenomenon of the Unspeakable. Whatever (Marcher feels) may be to be discovered along those lines, it is, in the view of his panic, *one* thing, and the worst thing, "the superstition of the Beast" (394). His readiness to organize the whole course of his life around the preparation for it—the defense against it—remakes his life monolithically in the image of *its* monolith of, in his view, the inseparability of homosexual desire, yielding, discovery, scandal, shame, annihilation. Finally, he has "but one desire left": that *it* be "decently proportional to the posture he had kept, all his life, in the threatened presence of it" (379).

This is how it happens that the outer secret, the secret of having a secret, functions, in Marcher's life, precisely as *the closet.* It is not a closet in which there is a homosexual man, for Marcher is not a homosexual man. Instead, however, it is the closet of, simply, the homosexual secret—the closet of imagining *a* homosexual secret. Yet it is unmistakable that Marcher lives as one who is *in the closet.* His angle on daily existence and intercourse is that of the closeted person,

> the secret of the difference between the forms he went through—those of his little office under government, those of caring for his modest patrimony, for his library, for his garden in the country, for the people in London whose invitations he accepted and repaid—and the detachment that reigned beneath them and that made of all behaviour, all that could in the least be called behaviour, a long act of dissimulation. What it had come to was that he wore a mask painted with the social simper, out of the eye-holes of which there looked eyes of an expression not in the least matching the other features. This the stupid world, even after years, had never more than half-discovered. (367–78)

Whatever the content of the inner secret, too, it is one whose protection requires, for him, a playacting of heterosexuality that is conscious of being only window dressing. "You help me," he tells May Bartram, "to pass for a man like another" (375). And "what saves us, you know," she explains, "is that we answer so completely to so usual an appearance: that of the man and woman whose friendship has become such a daily habit—or almost—as to be at last indispensable" (368-69). Oddly, they not only appear to be but are such a man and woman. The element of deceiving the world, of window dressing, comes into their relationship *only* because of the compulsion he feels to invest it with the legitimating stamp of visible, institutionalized genitality: "The real form it should have taken on the basis that stood out large was the form of their marrying. But the devil in this was that the very basis itself put marrying out of the question. His conviction, his apprehension, his obsession, in short, wasn't a privilege he could invite a woman to share; and that consequence of it was precisely what was the matter with him" (365).

Because of the terrified stultification of his fantasy about the inner or future secret, Marcher has, until the story's very last scene, an essentially static relation to and sense of both these secrets. Even the discovery that the outer secret is already shared with someone else, and the admission of May Bartram to the community it creates, "the dim day constituted by their discretions and privacies" (363), does nothing to his closet but furnish it—camouflage it to the eyes of outsiders, and soften its inner cushioning for his own comfort. In fact, the admission of May Bartram importantly *consolidates and fortifies* the closet for John Marcher.

In my hypothesis, however, May Bartram's view of Marcher's secrets is different from his and more fluid. I want to suggest that—while it is true that she feels desire for him—her involvement with him occurs originally on the ground of her understanding that he is imprisoned by homosexual panic; and her interest in his closet is not at all in helping him fortify it but in helping him dissolve it.

In this reading, May Bartram from the first sees, correctly, that the possibility of Marcher's achieving a genuine ability to attend to a woman—sexually or in any other way—depends as an absolute precondition on the dispersion of his totalizing, basilisk fascination with and terror of homosexual possibility. It is only through his coming out of the closet—whether as *a homosexual man*, or as a man with a less exclusively defined sexuality that nevertheless admits the possibility of desires for other men—that Marcher could even begin to perceive the attention of a woman as anything other than a terrifying demand or a devaluing complicity. The truth of this is already evident at the beginning of the story, in the surmises with which Marcher first meets May Bartram's allusion to something (he cannot remember what) he said to her years before: "The great thing was that he saw in this no vulgar reminder of any 'sweet' speech. The vanity of women had long memories, but she was making no claim on him of a compliment or a mistake. With another woman, a totally different one, he might have feared the recall possibly even of some imbecile 'offer'" (356). The alternative to this, however, in his eyes, is a different kind of "sweetness," that of a willingly shared confinement: "her knowledge . . . began, even if rather strangely, to taste sweet to him" (358). "Somehow the whole question was a new luxury to him—that is from the moment she was in possession. If she didn't take the sarcastic view she clearly took the sympathetic, and that was what he had had, in all the long time, from no one whomsoever. What he felt was that he couldn't at present have begun to tell her, and yet could profit perhaps exquisitely by the accident of having done so of old" (358). So begins the imprisonment of May Bartram in John Marcher's closet—an imprisonment that, the story makes explicit, is founded on his inability to perceive or value her as a person beyond her complicity in his view of his own predicament.

The conventional view of the story, emphasizing May Bartram's interest in liberating, unmediatedly, Marcher's heterosexual possibilities, would see her as unsuccessful in doing so until too late—until the true revelation that comes, however, only after her death. If what needs to be liberated is in the first place Marcher's potential for homosexual desire, however, the trajectory of the story must be seen as far bleaker. I hypothesize that what May Bartram would have liked for Marcher, the narrative she wished to nurture for him, would have been a progress from a vexed and gaping self-ignorance around his homosexual possibilities to a self-knowledge of them that would have freed him to find and enjoy a sexuality of whatever sort emerged. What she sees happen to Marcher, instead, is the "progress" that the culture more insistently enforces: the progress from a vexed and gaping self-ignorance around his homosexual possibilities, to a completed and rationalized and wholly concealed and accepted one. The moment of Marcher's full incorporation of his erotic self-ignorance is the moment at which the imperatives of the culture cease to enforce him, and he becomes instead the enforcer of the culture.

Section 4 of the story marks the moment at which May Bartram realizes that, far from helping dissolve Marcher's closet, she has instead and irremediably been permitting him to reinforce it. It is in this section and the next, too, that it becomes explicit in the story that Marcher's fate, what was to have happened to him and did happen, involves a change in him from being the suffering object of a Law or judgment (of a doom in the original sense of the word) to being the embodiment of that Law.

If the transition I am describing is, in certain respects, familiarly Oedipal, the structuring metaphor behind its description here seems to be oddly alimentative. The question that haunts Marcher in these sections is whether what he has thought of as the secret of his future may not be, after all, in the past; and the question of passing, of who is passing through what or what is passing through whom, of what residue remains to *be* passed, is the form in which he compulsively poses his riddle. Is the beast eating him, or is he eating the beast? "It hasn't passed you by," May Bartram tells him. "It has done its office. It has made you its own" (389). "It's past. It's behind, she finally tells him, to which he replies, "*Nothing*, for me, is past; nothing *will* pass till I pass myself, which I pray my stars may be as soon as possible. Say, however, . . . that I've eaten my cake, as you contend, to the last crumb—how can the thing I've never felt at all be the thing I was marked out to feel?" (391). What May Bartram sees, that Marcher does not, is that the process of incorporating— of embodying—the Law of masculine self-ignorance, is the one that has the least in the world to do with feeling.[32] To gape at and, rebelliously, be forced to swallow the Law is to feel; but to have it finally stick to one's ribs, become however incongruously a part of one's own organism, is then to perfect at the same moment a new hard-won insentience of it and an assumption of (or subsumption by) an identification with it. May Bartram answers Marcher's question, "You take your 'feelings' for granted. You were to suffer your fate. That was not necessarily to know it" (391). Marcher's fate is to cease to suffer fate, and, instead, to become it. May Bartram's fate, with the "slow fine shudder" that climaxes her ultimate appeal to Marcher, is herself to swallow this huge, bitter bolus with which *she* can have *no* deep identification, and to die of it—of what is, to her, knowledge, not power. "So on her lips would the law itself have sounded" (389). Or, tasted.

To end a reading of May Bartram with her death, to end with her silenced forever in that ultimate closet, "her" tomb that represents (to Marcher) *his fate,* would be to do to her feminine desire the same thing I have already argued that James M. Barrie, unforgivably, did to Grizel's. That is to say, it leaves us in danger of figuring May Bartram, or more generally the woman in heterosexuality, as only the exact, heroic supplement to the murderous enforcements of male homophobic/homosocial self-ignorance. "The Fox," Emily Dickinson wrote, "fits the Hound."[33] It would be only too easy to describe May Bartram as the fox that most irreducibly fits this particular hound. She seems the woman (don't we all know them?) who has not only the most delicate nose for but the most potent attraction toward men who are at crises of homosexual panic . . . —Though for that matter, won't most women admit that an arousing nimbus, an excessively refluent and dangerous maelstrom of eroticism, somehow attends men in general at such moments, even otherwise boring men?

If one is to avoid the Barrie-ism of describing May Bartram in terms that reduce her perfectly to the residue-less sacrifice John Marcher makes to his Beast, it might be by inquiring into the difference of the paths of her own desire. What does she want— not for him, but for herself—from their relationship? What does she actually get? To speak less equivocally from my own eros and experience, there is a particular relation to truth and authority that a mapping of male homosexual panic offers to a woman in the emotional vicinity. The fact that male heterosexual entitlement in (at least modern Anglo-American) culture depends on a perfected but always friable self-ignorance in men as to the significance of their desire for other men, means that it is always open to women to know something that it is much more dangerous for any nonhomosexual-identified man to know. The ground of May Bartram's and John Marcher's relationship from the first is that she has the advantage of him, cognitively: she remembers, as he does not, where and when and with whom they have met before, and most of all she remembers his "secret" from a decade ago while he forgets having told it to her. This differential of knowledge affords her a "slight irony," an "advantage" (353)—but one that he can at the same time use to his own profit as "the buried treasure of her knowledge," "this little hoard" (363). As their relationship continues, the sense of power and of a marked, rather free-floating irony about May Bartram becomes stronger and stronger, even in proportion to Marcher's accelerating progress toward self-ignorance and toward a blindly selfish expropriation of her emotional labor. Both the care and the creativity of her investment in him, the imaginative reach of her fostering his homosexual potential as a route back to his truer perception of herself, are forms of gender-political resilience in her as well as of love. They are forms of excitement, too, of real though insufficient power, and of pleasure.

In the last scene of the "The Beast in the Jungle," John Marcher becomes, in this reading, not the finally self-knowing man who is capable of heterosexual love, but the irredeemably self-ignorant man who embodies and enforces heterosexual compulsion. In this reading, that is to say, May Bartram's prophecy to Marcher that "You'll never know now" (390) is *a true one*.

Importantly for the homosexual plot, too, the final scene is also the only one in the entire story that reveals or tests the affective quality of Marcher's perception of another man. "The shock of the face" (399)—this is, in the last scene, the beginning of what Marcher ultimately considers "the most extraordinary thing that had happened to him" (400). At the beginning of Marcher's confrontation with this male figure at the cemetery, the erotic possibilities of the connection between the men appear to be all open. The man, whose "mute assault" Marcher feels "so deep down that he winced at the steady thrust," is mourning profoundly over "a grave apparently fresh," but (perhaps only to Marcher's closet-sharpened suspicions?) a slightest potential of Whitmanian cruisiness seems at first to tinge the air, as well.

> His pace was slow, so that—and all the more as there was a kind of hunger in his look—the two men were for a minute directly confronted. Marcher knew him at once for one of the deeply stricken . . . nothing lived but the deep ravage of the features he showed. He *showed* them— that was the point; he was moved, as he passed, by some impulse that was either a signal for sympathy or, more possibly, a challenge to an

opposed sorrow. He might already have been aware of our friend. . . .
What Marcher was at all events conscious of was in the first place that
the image of scarred passion presented to him was conscious too—of
something that profaned the air; and in the second that, roused, startled,
shocked, he was yet the next moment looking after it, as it went, with
envy. (400–401)

The path traveled by Marcher's desire in this brief and cryptic
non-encounter reenacts a classic trajectory of male entitlement.
Marcher begins with the possibility of *desire for* the man, in
response to the man's open "hunger" ("which," afterward,
"still flared for him like a smoky torch" [401]). Deflecting that
desire under a fear of profanation, he then replaces it with envy,
with an *identification with* the man in that man's (baffled) desire
for some other, female, dead object. "The stranger passed, but
the raw glare of his grief remained, making our friend wonder
in pity what wrong, what wound it expressed, what injury not
to be healed. What had the man *had,* to make him by the loss of
it so bleed and yet live?" (401).

What had the man *had?* The loss by which a man *so bleeds
and yet lives* is, is it not, supposed to be the castratory one of
the phallus figured as mother, the inevitability of whose sacrifice
ushers sons into the status of fathers and into the control (read
both ways) of the Law. What is strikingly open in the ending of
"The Beast in the Jungle" is how central to that process is man's
desire for man—and the denial of that desire. The imperative
that there *be* a male figure to take this place is the clearer in
that, at an earlier climactic moment, in a female "shock of the
face," May Bartram has presented to Marcher her own face, in
a conscious revelation that was far more clearly of desire.

It had become suddenly, from her movement and attitude, beautiful
and vivid to him that she had something more to give him; her wasted
face delicately shone with it—it glittered almost as with the white
lustre of silver in her expression. She was right, incontestably, for what
he saw in her face was the truth, and strangely, without consequence,
while their talk of it as dreadful was still in the air, she appeared to

> present it as inordinately soft. This, prompting bewilderment, made him but gape the more gratefully for her revelation, so that they continued for some minutes silent, her face shining at him, her contact imponderably pressing, and his stare all kind but all expectant. The end, none the less, was that what he had expected failed to come to him. (386)

To the shock of the female face, Marcher is not phobic but simply numb. It is only by turning his desire for the male face into an envious identification with male loss that Marcher finally comes into *any* relation to a woman—and then it is a relation through one dead woman (the other man's) to another dead woman of his own. That is to say, it is the relation of *compulsory* heterosexuality.

When Lytton Strachey's claim to be a conscientious objector was being examined, he was asked what he would do if a German were to try to rape his sister. "I should," he is said to have replied, "try and interpose my own body." [34] Not the gay self-knowledge but the heterosexual, self-ignorant acting out of just this fantasy ends "The Beast in the Jungle." To face the gaze of the Beast would have been, for Marcher, to dissolve it. [35] To face the "kind of hunger in the look" of the grieving man—to explore at all into the sharper lambencies of that encounter—would have been to dissolve the closet. Marcher, instead, to the very end, turns his back—re-creating a double scenario of homosexual compulsion and heterosexual compulsion. "He saw the Jungle of his life and saw the lurking Beast; then, while he looked, perceived it, as by a stir of the air, rise, huge and hideous, for the leap that was to settle him. His eyes darkened—it was close; and, instinctively turning, in his hallucination, to avoid it, he flung himself, face down, on the tomb" (402).

NOTES

This essay has profited—though not as fully as I wish I had been able to make it do—from especially helpful readings by Maud Ellmann, Neil Hertz, H. A. Sedgwick, D. A. Miller, and Ruth Bernard Yeazell.

1. Lawrence to Jessie Chambers, Aug. 1910, *The Collected Letters of D. H. Lawrence,* ed. Harry T. Moore (London: W. H. Heinemann, 1962), 1: 63.

2. Lawrence to Rolf Gardiner, Aug. 9, 1924, in ibid. 2: 801.

3. Alan Bray, *Homosexuality in Renaissance England* (London: Gay Men's Press, 1982), chs. 1–3. Note the especially striking example on pp. 68–69, 76–77.

4. Ibid., p. 25.

5. Eve Kosofsky Sedgwick, *Between Men: English Literature and Male Homosocial Desire* (New York: Columbia University Press, 1985), pp. 83–96.

6. Claude Lévi-Strauss, *The Elementary Structures of Kinship* (Boston: Beacon Press, 1969), p. 115; also quoted and well discussed in Gayle Rubin, "The Traffic in Women: Notes Toward a Political Economy of Sex," in *Toward an Anthropology of Women,* ed. Rayna Reiter (New York: Monthly Review Press, 1975), pp. 157–210.

7. Heidi Hartmann, "The Unhappy Marriage of Marxism and Feminism: Towards a More Progressive Union," in *Women and Revolution: A Discussion of the Unhappy Marriage of Marxism and Feminism,* ed. Lydia Sargent (Boston: South End Press, 1981), p. 14; emphasis added.

8. Bray, *Homosexuality,* ch. 4.

9. Sedgwick, *Between Men,* pp. 88–89.

10. By "paranoid Gothic" I mean Romantic novels in which a male hero is in a close, usually murderous relation to another male figure, in some respects his "double," to whom he seems to be mentally transparent. Examples of the paranoid Gothic include, besides *Frankenstein,* Ann Radcliffe's *The Italian,* William Godwin's *Caleb Williams,* and James Hogg's *Confessions of a Justified Sinner.* This tradition is discussed more fully in my *Between Men,* chs. 5 and 6.

11. Sigmund Freud, "Psycho-Analytic Notes on an Autobiographical Account of a Case of Paranoia (Dementia Paranoides)," in *The Standard Edition of the Complete Psychological Works of Sigmund Freud,* trans. and ed. James Strachey et al. (London: Hogarth Press, 1953–73), 12: 143–77.

12. On this see, along with Bray, *Homosexuality,* such works as John Boswell, *Christianity, Social Tolerance, and Homosexuality: Gay People in Western Europe from the Beginning of the Christian Era to the Fourteenth Century* (Chicago: University of Chicago Press, 1980); Jonathan Katz, *A Gay/Lesbian Almanac* (New York: Thomas Y. Crowell Co., 1982); Jeffrey Weeks, *Coming Out: Homosexual Politics in Britain from the Nineteenth Century to the Present* (London: Quartet Books, 1977);

and Weeks, *Sex, Politics, and Society: The Regulation of Sexuality since 1800* (London: Longman & Co., 1981).

13. For more on bachelors see Frederic Jameson, *Wyndham Lewis: Fables of Aggression* (Berkeley and Los Angeles: University of California Press, 1979), ch. 2; also, cited in Jameson, Jean Borie, *Le Célibataire français* (Paris: Le Sagittaire, 1976); and Edward Said, *Beginnings* (New York: Basic Books, 1975), pp. 137–52.

14. F. O. Matthiessen and Kenneth B. Murdock, eds., *The Notebooks of Henry James* (New York: Oxford University Press, 1947), p. 28.

15. Bachelor literature in which the paranoid Gothic—or more broadly, the supernatural—makes a reappearance includes, besides Du Maurier's *Trilby*, George Eliot's *The Lifted Veil*, Robert Louis Stevenson's *Dr. Jekyll and Mr. Hyde*, numerous Kipling stories such as "In the Same Boat," and numerous James stories such as "The Jolly Corner."

16. *Lovel the Widower*, in *Works of Thackeray* (New York: National Library, n.d.), 1: ch. 1. Subsequent references to this novel are to this edition and are cited parenthetically in the text by chapter number.

17. In, respectively, Trollope's *The Claverings* and Thackeray's *Pendennis* and *Vanity Fair;* "Soapey" Sponge is in R. S. Surtees's *Mr. Sponge's Sporting Tour.*

18. Richard Miller, *Bohemia: The Protoculture Then and Now* (Chicago: Nelson-Hall Co., 1977), p. 58.

19. *Notebooks of James,* Matthiessen and Murdock, eds., pp. 97–98.

20. "Ballads," *Works of Thackeray* 6: 337.

21. George Du Maurier, *Trilby* (New York: Harper & Bros., 1922), p. 271.

22. The effect of emboldenment should be to some extent mistrusted—not, I think, because the attribution to these particular figures of a knowledge of male homosexual panic is likely to be wrong, but because it is so much easier to be so emboldened about men who are arguably homosexual in (if such a thing exists) "basic" sexual orientation; while what I am arguing is that panic is proportioned not to the homosexual but to the nonhomosexual-identified elements of these men's characters. Thus, if Barrie and James are obvious authors with whom to *begin* an analysis of male homosexual panic, the analysis I am offering here must be inadequate to the degree that it does not work just as well—even better—for Joyce, Milton, Faulkner, Lawrence, Yeats.

23. Leon Edel, *Henry James: The Middle Years: 1882–1895*, vol. 3 of *The Life of Henry James* (New York: J. B. Lippincott, Co., 1962; repr., Avon Books, 1978), makes clear that these contacts—coinciding visits to some cities and shared trips to others (e.g., 3: 94), "a special rendezvous" in Geneva (3: 217), a period of actually living in the same house (3:

215-17)—were conducted with a consistent and most uncharacteristic extreme of secrecy. (James seems also to have taken extraordinary pains to destroy every vestige of his correspondence with Woolson.) Edel cannot, nevertheless, imagine the relationship except as "a continuing 'virtuous' attachment": "That this pleasant and *méticuleuse* old maid may have nourished fantasies of a closer tie does not seem to have occurred to him at this time. If it had, we might assume he would have speedily put distance between himself and her" (3: 217). Edel's hypothesis does nothing, of course, to explain the secrecy of these and other meetings.

24. Edel, *Life of James*, vol. 4, *The Master: 1910-1916*, pp. 132-40.

25. "The Beast in the Jungle," in *The Complete Tales of Henry James*, ed. Leon Edel (London: Rupert Hart-Davis, 1964), 11:401. All subsequent references to this work are to this edition and are cited parenthetically in the text by page number.

26. Interestingly, in the 1895 germ of (what seems substantially to be) "The Beast in the Jungle," in James's *Notebooks*, p. 184, the woman outlives the man. "It's *the woman's sense of what might [have been] in him* that arrives at the intensity. . . . *She is his Dead Self: he is alive in her and dead in himself*—that is something like the little formula I seem to *entrevoir*. He himself, the man, must, *in* the tale, also materially die—die in the flesh as he has died long ago in the spirit, the *right* one. Then it is that his lost treasure revives most—no longer *contrarié* by his material existence, existence in his false self, his wrong one."

27. Quoted in Boswell, *Christianity*, p. 349 (from a legal document dated 533) and p. 380 (from a 1227 letter from Pope Honorious III).

28. Quoted in Bray, *Homosexuality*—the first two from p. 61 (from Edward Coke's *Institutes* and Sir David Lindsay's *Works*), the next two from p. 62 (from William Bradford's *Plimouth Plantation* and Guillaume Du Bartas's *Divine Weeks*), and the last from p. 22, also from Du Bartas.

29. Lord Alfred Douglas, "Two Loves," from *The Chameleon*, quoted in Byron R. S. Fone, *Hidden Heritage: History and the Gay Imagination* (New York: Irvington Publishers, 1981), p. 196.

30. For a striking anecdotal example of the mechanism of this, see Beverley Nichols, *Father Figure* (New York: Simon & Schuster, 1972), pp. 92-99.

31. Exceptions that I know of include Georges-Michel Sarotte's discussions of James in *Like a Brother, Like a Lover: Male Homosexuality in the American Novel and Theater from Herman Melville to James Baldwin*, trans. Richard Miller (New York: Doubleday & Co. / Anchor, 1978); Richard Hall, "Henry James: Interpreting an Obsessive Memory," *Journal of Homosexuality* 8, no. 3 / 4 (Spring / Summer 1983): 83-97; and Robert

K. Martin, "The 'High Felicity' of Comradeship: A New Reading of Roderick Hudson," *American Literary Realism* 11 (Spring 1978): 100–108.

32. A fascinating passage in James's *Notebooks,* p. 318, written in 1905 in California, shows how a greater self-knowledge in James, and a greater acceptance and *specificity* of homosexual desire, transform this half-conscious enforcing rhetoric of anality, numbness, and silence into a much richer, pregnant address to James's male muse, an invocation of fisting-as-*écriture*:

> *I sit here, after long weeks, at any rate, in front of my arrears, with an inward accumulation of material of which I feel the wealth, and as to which I can only invoke my familiar demon of patience, who always comes, doesn't he?, when I call. He is here with me in front of this cool green Pacific—he sits close and I feel his soft breath, which cools and steadies and inspires, on my cheek. Everything sinks in: nothing is lost; everything abides and fertilizes and renews its golden promise, making me think with closed eyes of deep and grateful longing when, in the full summer days of L[amb] H[ouse], my long dusty adventure over, I shall be able to [plunge] my hand, my arm, in, deep and far, and up to the shoulder—into the heavy bag of remembrance—of suggestion— of imagination—of art—and fish out every little figure and felicity, every little fact and fancy that can be to my purpose. These things are all packed away, now, thicker than I can penetrate, deeper than I can fathom, and there let them rest for the present, in their sacred cool darkness, till I shall let in upon them the mild still light of dear old L[amb] H[ouse]—in which they will begin to gleam and glitter and take form like the gold and jewels of a mine.*

33. *Collected Poems of Emily Dickinson,* ed. Thomas H. Johnson (Boston: Little, Brown & Co., 1960), p. 406.

34. Lytton Strachey, quoted in Michael Holroyd, *Lytton Strachey: A Critical Biography* (London: W. H. Heinemann, 1968), 2: 179.

35. Ruth Bernard Yeazell makes clear the oddity of having Marcher turn his back on the Beast that is supposed, at this late moment, to represent his self-recognition (in *Language and Knowledge in the Late Novels of Henry James* [Chicago: University of Chicago Press, 1976], pp. 37–38).

The English Institute, 1984

The Program

Friday, August 31, through Monday, September 3, 1984

I. Another American Renaissance: Harlem in the Roaring Twenties
    Directed by Barbara Johnson, Harvard University
    Fri. 2 P.M.   Self-Reflection and Comparative American
                     Literature: Zora Neale Hurston's *Mules and
                     Men*
                     Barbara Johnson, Harvard University
    Sat. 9:30 A.M.   A Question of Power: Jessie Fauset, Horizons
                     of Expectation, and the Literature of the
                     Harlem Renaissance
                     Deborah McDowell, Colby College
    Sat. 11 A.M.   The "New" Negro: The Trope of Reconstruction
                     Henry Louis Gates, Jr., Yale University

II. The Lyric Spenser
    Directed by Paul Alpers, University of California, Berkeley
    Fri. 3:30 P.M.   Pastoral and the Domain of Lyric
                     Paul Alpers, University of California, Berkeley
    Sat. 2 P.M.   Spenser's Undersong
                     John Hollander, Yale University
    Sat. 3:30 P.M.   Suspended Instruments
                     *Patricia Parker, Victoria College, University of
                     Toronto*

III. The Hebrew Bible: Sacred Text and Secular Interpretation
    Directed by Geoffrey Hartman, Yale University
    Sun. 9:30 A.M.   Poetic Form and Religious Experience in Psalms
                     Robert Alter, University of California, Berkeley
    Sun. 11 A.M.   The Double Cave: Biblical Naming and Poetic
                     Etymology
                     Herbert Marks, Indiana University, Bloomington
    Mon. 9:30 A.M.   The Garments of Torah—To What May Scripture
                     Be Likened?
                     Michael Fishbane, Brandeis University

Mon. 11 A.M.   The Struggle for the Text
                     Geoffrey Hartman, Yale University

IV. New Perspectives on the Nineteenth-Century Novel
    Directed by Ruth Bernard Yeazell, University of California, Los Angeles

Sun. 2 P.M.   The Perils of Observation: Scientific Ideal and
                     Narrative Practice in Victorian Fiction
                     George Levine, Rutgers University
Sun. 3:30 P.M.   Origins and Oblivion in Victorian Narrative
                     *Gillian Beer, Girton College, Cambridge
                     University*
Mon. 2 P.M.   Trollope: The Novel as Usual
                     D. A. Miller, University of California, Berkeley
Mon. 3:30 P.M.   Alluring Vacancies in the Victorian Character
                     Nina Auerbach, University of Pennsylvania

Sponsoring Institutions

Columbia University, Princeton University, Yale University, University of Rochester, Claremont Graduate School, Rutgers University, Michigan State University, Northwestern University, Boston University, University of California, Berkeley, University of Connecticut, Harvard University, University of Pennsylvania, University of Virginia, Amherst College, Brandeis University, Cornell University, Dartmouth College, New York University, Smith College, The Johns Hopkins University, Washington University, State University of New York at Albany, Temple University, University of Alabama in Birmingham, University of California, San Diego, Boston College, Brigham Young University, University of California, Los Angeles, Massachusetts Institute of Technology, Wellesley College, Stanford University, Indiana University, Bloomington, Tufts University, University of Colorado, Wesleyan University, Fordham University, State University of New York at Buffalo, University of California, Irvine, University of Maryland, University of Miami, Emory University, University of Illinois at Chicago, University of California, Riverside, University of Tulsa, University of Southern California, Ohio State University, University of Massachusetts—Amherst, The New York Public Library, University of Minnesota

Registrants, 1984

Tim Abraham, New York City Board of Education; Meena Alexander, Fordham University; Marcia Allentuck, City University of New York; Paul Alpers, University of California, Berkeley; Robert Alpert, Boston College; Robert Alter, University of California, Berkeley; Vincent Anderson, North Park College; Jonathan Arac, University of Illinois at Chicago; N. S. Asbridge, Central Connecticut State University; Nina Auerbach, University of Pennsylvania; Henry Auster, University of Toronto

George W. Bahlke, Hamilton College; Houston Baker, University of Pennsylvania; Carol Barash, Princeton University; J. Robert Barth, S.J., University of Missouri—Columbia; James F. Beaton, Middlesex School; Jerome

Beaty, Emory University; Gillian Beer, Girton College, Cambridge University; Elizabeth J. Bellamy, University of Alabama in Birmingham; Nancy M. Bentley, La Jolla School; Adele Berlin, University of Maryland; Jerry Bernhard, Emmanuel College; Marilyn E. Bersh, Yale University; Don Bialostosky, State University of New York at Stony Brook; Morton W. Bloomfield, Harvard University; Charles Blyth, Cambridge, Mass.; Anne Bolgan, University of Western Ontario; Zelda Boyd, California State University, Hayward; Frank Brady, City University of New York Graduate Center; Peter Brand, Buffalo and Erie County Public Library; Leo Braudy, University of Southern California; Leslie Brisman, Yale University; Audrey Brune, Concordia University; Jane Buchanan, Tufts University; John Burt, Brandeis University; Ronald Bush, California Institute of Technology

Ruth A. Cameron, Eastern Nazarene College; Mary Wilson Carpenter, Harvard University; Stanley Cavell, Harvard University; Nathan A. Cervo, Franklin Pierce College; Donald Cheney, University of Massachusetts; Ralph Cohen, University of Virginia; Robert A. Coles, Fordham University; Arthur N. Collins, State University of New York at Albany; Patricia Craddock, Boston University; Jonathan Culler, Cornell University

David Damrosch, Columbia University; Winifred M. Davis, Columbia University; Joanne Dempsey, University of San Diego; Morris Dickstein, Queens College, City University of New York; Deborah Dobrusin, Columbia University; E. T. Donaldson, Indiana University, Bloomington; Philomene Ducas, Eastern Connecticut State University; Edward Duffy, Marquette University

David V. Erdman, State University of New York at Stony Brook

Blossom Feinstein, C. W. Post College, Long Island University; Peter Fellowes, North Park College; N. N. Feltes, York University; Frances Ferguson, University of California, Berkeley; Margaret Ferguson, Yale University; Mary Anne Ferguson, University of Massachusetts—Boston; Michael Fishbane, Brandeis University; Philip Fisher, Brandeis University; Marcia Folsom, Wheelock College; Debra Fried, Cornell University; Michael Fried, The Johns Hopkins University; Everett Frost, Chelsea, Mass.; Lowell T. Frye/Elizabeth J. Deis; Margaretta Fulton, Harvard University Press

Catherine Gallagher, University of California, Berkeley; Marjorie Garber, Harvard University; Burdett Gardner, West Long Branch, N.J.; Henry Louis Gates, Jr., Yale University; Edward A. Geary, Brigham Young University; Blanche H. Gelfant, Dartmouth College; William P. Germano, Columbia University Press; Janet K. Gezari, Connecticut College; Lissa Gifford, Brandeis University; Harry Girling, York University; Sandor Goodheart, University of Michigan; Norman S. Grabo, University of Tulsa; Edward Graham, State University of New York Maritime College; Kenneth Gross, University of Rochester; Allen Grossman, Brandeis University

Pauline Harrison, University of Cincinnati; Geoffrey Hartman, Yale University; Joan E. Hartman, College of Staten Island, City University of New York; Dayton Haskin, Boston College; Peter S. Hawkins, Yale University; Harris M. Heath, Fairfield County Schools; Carolyn Heilbrun, Columbia University; Neil Hertz, The Johns Hopkins University; Iain Higgins, Harvard University; Margaret Higgonet, University of Connecticut; Eugene Hollahan, Georgia State University; John Hollander, Yale University; Susan R. Horton, University of Massachusetts—Boston; Susan E. Houchins, Scripps College; Peter Hughes, Universitaet Zürich; J. Paul Hunter, University of Rochester

Mary Jacobus, Cornell University; Rachel Jacoff, Wellesley College; Anne F. Janowitz, Brandeis University; Barbara Johnson, Harvard University; Richard A. Johnson, Mount Holyoke College; Kenneth R. Johnston, Indiana University, Bloomington; Gerhard Joseph, Lehman College / City University of New York Graduate Center; Claire Kahane, State University of New York at Buffalo; Jonathan Kamholtz/Sally Hoffheimer, University of Cincinnati; Robert Kern, Boston College; Christopher Klahre, Boston College; Jon Klancher, California Institute of Technology; J. Douglas Kneale, Yale University

G. P. Lair, Delbarton School; Ellen Landcrest, Boston University; Berel Lang, State University of New York at Albany; Vivien Leonard, Rensselaer Polytechnic Institute; George Levine, Rutgers University; Herbert J. Levine, Franklin and Marshall College; Alan Levitan, Brandeis University; John L'Heureux, Stanford University; Kathryne V. Lindberg, Harvard University; Joanna Lipking, Northwestern University; Michelle Carbone Loris, Sacred Heart University; Joseph P. Lovering, Canisius College

Pamela McCallum, University of Calgary; Nellie McKay, University of Wisconsin, Madison; Bruce McKenna, Brandeis University; Hugh MacLean, State University of New York at Albany; Cathleen T. McLoughlin, City University of New York Graduate Center; Capt. John B. Mahon, United States Coast Guard Academy; Cristina Malcomson, Yale University; Darrel

Mansell, Dartmouth College; Herbert Marks, Indiana University; Robert K. Martin, Concordia University; Donald C. Mell, University of Delaware; Dorothee Metlitzki, Yale Universtiy; D. A. Miller, University of California, Berkeley; Dorothy Miller, Boston College; Steven Mullaney, Massachusetts Institute of Technology

John Nesselhof, Wells College

Charles A. Owen, Jr., University of Connecticut

Barbara Packer, University of California, Los Angeles; Stanley R. Palumbo, George Washington University; Patricia Parker, Victoria College; Coleman O. Parsons, City University of New York; Ruth Perry, Massachusetts Institute of Technology; Vincent Petronella, University of Massachusetts—Boston; Leslie Phillips, Suffolk University; Diana Postlethwaite, Mount Holyoke College; Robert O. Preyer, Brandeis University; Janice Price, Methuen, Inc.; John W. Price, Middlesex School

David Quint, Princeton University

Dennis Radford, Atlantic Union College; Gail Reimer, Wellesley College; Louis A. Renza, Dartmouth; Marilyn Richardson, Massachusetts Institute of Technology; Robert D. Richardson, University of Denver; Julie Rivkin, Connecticut College; Bruce Robbins, Rutgers University; Alan Rosen, Boston University; Philip C. Rule, S. J., College of the Holy Cross; Adelaide M. Russo, Harvard University; John Paul Russo, University of Miami

Phillips Salman, Cleveland State University; Elaine Scarry, University of Pennsylvania; Sue Schopf, Harvard University; Eve Kosofsky Sedgwick, Amherst College; Mark Seltzer, Cornell University; Elaine Showalter, Rutgers University; Maeera Shreiber, Brandeis University; Lauren Silberman, Baruch College, City University of New York; Carole Silver, Yeshiva University; Mark D. Slown, United States Air Force Academy; Anita Sokolsky, Williams College; Ian Sowton, York University; Michael Sprinker, State University of New York at Stony Brook; Holly Stevens, Guilford, Conn.; Richard Stevenson, University of Oregon; Margaret Storch, Bentley College; Richard Strier, University of Chicago

John S. Tanner, Brigham Young University; Irene Tayler, Massachusetts Institute of Technology; Dennis Taylor, Boston College; Gordon O. Taylor, University of Tulsa; Elizabeth Tenenbaum; Herbert Lehman College, City

University of New York; David Thorburn, Massachusetts Institute of Technology; Stephen Tifft, Yale University; J. J. M. Tobin, University of Massachusetts—Boston; Lewis A. Turlish, Bates College

Helen Vendler, Boston University and Harvard University; Nancy J. Vickers, Dartmouth College

Melissa G. Walker, Mercer University; Jerome T. Walsh, St. John's Seminary; Rosanna Warren, Boston University; Thayer S. Warshaw, Indiana University, Bloomington; Mary Helen Washington, University of Massachusetts—Boston; Lindsay Waters, Harvard University Press; Sister Mary Anthony Weinig, Rosemont College; Epi Wiese, Cambridge, Mass.; Maud Wilcox, Harvard University Press; Joshua Wilner, Hebrew University; Judith Wilt, Boston College; Susan Winnett, Harvard University; Susanne L. Wofford, Yale University; Michael Wolff, University of Massachusetts, Amherst

Patricia Yaeger, Harvard University; Richard Yarborough, University of California, Los Angeles; Ruth Bernard Yeazell, University of California, Los Angeles